HAL LEONARD KEYBOARD STYLE SERIES

GOSPEL PIANO

THE COMPLETE GUIDE WITH AUDIO!

To access audio visit:
www.halleonard.com/mylibrary

Enter Code
7647-7398-7301-6672

BY KURT COWLING

ISBN 978-1-4234-1249-6

HAL•LEONARD®
CORPORATION

7777 W. BLUEMOUND RD. P.O. BOX 13819 MILWAUKEE, WI 53213

In Australia Contact:
Hal Leonard Australia Pty. Ltd.
4 Lentara Court
Cheltenham, Victoria, 3192 Australia
Email: ausadmin@halleonard.com

Visit Hal Leonard Online at www.halleonard.com

INTRODUCTION

If you flip through the AM radio dial in any large city in the U.S., you can almost always find a station that plays gospel music. You recognize it as soon as you hear it. The band is cookin'; there's a lead singer going all-out, and the choir is responding in three-part harmony, with what sounds like at least a hundred voices! You might not even need to hear the lyrics to know that it's gospel music. I'm talking about the gospel music found in many African-American churches today: the gospel music that started way back with the 19th and early 20th century hymns by Charles A. Tindley and later Thomas A. Dorsey (who added the blues influence). It came through the era of the great gospel quartets and solo artists of the mid-twentieth century, and in the 1980s emerged into the era of the "mass choir." Combining it with R&B, funk, and jazz has expanded it even more in the last decade.

Gospel music marked a radical change in church music. The lyrics were more about personal everyday struggles, triumphs, and encouragement that demonstrated faith and forgiveness, rather than about pure theological concepts. In the same way, the melodies, harmonies, and rhythms needed to be catchy and easily remembered by everyone (not just by those who could read music). Gospel music, like jazz and blues, is one of the true American art forms.

Who Is This Book For?

Since this book relies heavily upon written musical examples, it is intended mostly for those who have fairly strong reading skills. That may seem odd since gospel music is largely an "oral/aural" tradition. There are several courses about gospel music that rely heavily on visuals (i.e., a DVD with hands playing on a keyboard). Those are intended for people who already play gospel music (mostly by ear), but are looking for some new material to add to their bag of tricks. Conversely, this book and audio are geared toward a musician who has had some formal music training, is familiar with chord symbols, and perhaps plays in their church, but who hasn't had much exposure to gospel music.

About the Audio

On the accompanying audio you'll find demonstrations of nearly every musical example in the book. The examples from Chapter 8 include a rhythm section (bass and drums) as well.

About the Author

Kurt Cowling has been playing gospel music for the last ten years with an inner-city gospel choir. He also tours as pianist/conductor with the vocal jazz group Five By Design.

He has performed for the past 25 years across North America, as well as in Europe, the Caribbean, and China. Kurt is an award-winning composer of commercial music for advertising, and also produces music and sound design for theatrical productions.

CONTENTS

Chapter 1

OVERVIEW OF CHORDS AND CHORD SYMBOLS

Much of what gives gospel music its unique sound is the way it uses harmony and chord progressions. This quick overview of chord construction and chord symbols will help you to get the most out of the following chapters. This chapter assumes that you know your major and minor scales (along with their key signatures), and understand intervals (i.e., major third, minor seventh).

Basic Three-note Chords (Triads)

Gospel music is like much other Western music in that it uses **triads** (three-note chords) as the smallest "complete" unit of harmony. Single notes (unisons) and two-note chords (dyads) are certainly possible, but they always constitute incomplete versions of larger chords with at least three notes (and very possibly more). Because of this, the gospel pianist must be well versed in triads; they are the building blocks of more complex chords.

Triad Formation and Inversions

We create triads by adding a third and a fifth above a fundamental note (called the root). This can be done with each note in a major or minor scale. Here we see triads built on each note of the C major scale. You can also think of this as "stacking" two thirds, one atop the other.

Root position:

In each of the eight triads above, the bottom note is the root, the middle note is the third, and the top note is the fifth. This arrangement, with the root on the bottom, is known as **root position**. It's also possible to "flip," or **invert** the order of the notes as follows:

First inversion:

We've moved each root up an octave, while leaving the third and fifth where they were. This arrangement, with the third on the bottom, is known as **first inversion**. With a three-note chord we can invert the order one more time:

Second inversion:

Now both the root and the third are an octave higher than where they started. This arrangement, in which the fifth is on the bottom, is called (you guessed it!) **second inversion**. If we tried to invert this one more time, we would simply be back to root position again (but with everything an octave higher than before).

Now let's look at this in another key. Here are the root-position triads in the key of B♭ major. They're built the same way as in the key of C major, by placing a third and a fifth above each note of the B♭ major scale. You simply need to observe the key signature to make it sound in B♭ major:

You'll notice as you play through these that some chords have a brighter sound and some a darker sound. That's because some are major chords (the brighter sounding ones) and some are minor chords (the darker ones). There is even one diminished chord. A closer look at the intervals, especially the third, will explain why. (Remember: I said you'd need to know your intervals!)

Chord Quality and Scale Degrees

Here are just the root and the third for each note of the B♭ major scale. They are marked above the staff with the interval **quality**, in this case major (M) or minor (m). The numbers below the staff indicate the **scale degree**, or position within the scale (1st note, 2nd note, 3rd note, etc.). Notice that the last pair is the same as the first, but an octave higher. Notice also that the major 3rds occur on the 1st, 4th, and 5th scale degrees. All of the others are minor 3rds.

Now we'll add the fifths back in and see what happens:

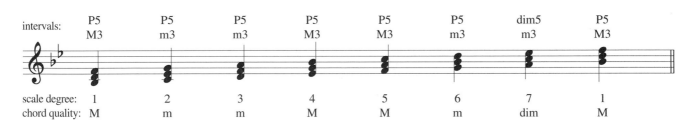

Well, all the 5ths except one are perfect 5ths. The combination of a root, a major 3rd, and a perfect 5th creates a **major triad**. The combination of a root, a minor 3rd, and a perfect 5th creates a **minor triad**. On the 7th scale degree we have the combination of a minor 3rd and a diminished 5th (essentially two stacked minor 3rds) creating a **diminished triad**. This distinction between major, minor, and diminished is known as the **quality** of a chord. You'll see in the above example that major triads are found with roots on the 1st, 4th, and 5th scale degrees. Minor triads are found with roots on the 2nd, 3rd, and 6th scale degrees. The triad found on the 7th scale degree is diminished. This is true for all major scales.

Using Roman Numerals

When talking about the quality of a chord and the scale degree of its root, we can combine the two pieces of information by using upper- and lowercase Roman numerals.

The Roman numeral itself indicates the scale degree of the root, and upper- or lowercase tells us the quality (uppercase for major, lowercase for minor, and lowercase followed by a small circle indicating diminished). This helps us identify the chords even when they come in a different order and are in different inversions.

TRACK 1

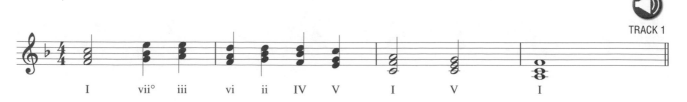

| I | vii° | iii | vi | ii | IV | V | I | V | I |

Using Letter Names

We can also name chords by the letter name of the root rather than by scale degree. In this case, we use all uppercase letters for the letter name and add a lowercase "m" to signify minor, or a small circle to indicate diminished.

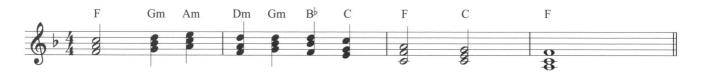

| F | Gm | Am | Dm | Gm | B♭ | C | F | C | F |

Minor-key Triads

We can do the same thing in a minor key, although things are complicated somewhat by the fact that there are three slightly different minor scales (natural, harmonic, and melodic). Also notice that we get one new type of triad, the augmented triad, which has a major 3rd and an augmented 5th.

Natural minor scale

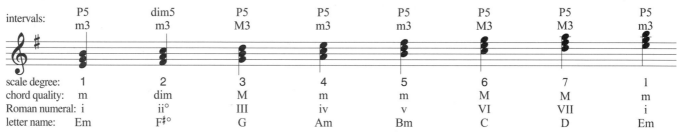

intervals:	P5 m3	dim5 m3	P5 M3	P5 m3	P5 m3	P5 M3	P5 M3	P5 m3
scale degree:	1	2	3	4	5	6	7	1
chord quality:	m	dim	M	m	m	M	M	m
Roman numeral:	i	ii°	III	iv	v	VI	VII	i
letter name:	Em	F♯°	G	Am	Bm	C	D	Em

Harmonic minor scale

intervals:	P5 m3	dim5 m3	aug5 M3	P5 m3	P5 M3	P5 M3	dim5 m3	P5 m3
scale degree:	1	2	3	4	5	6	♯7	1
chord quality:	m	dim	aug	m	M	M	dim	m
Roman numeral:	i	ii°	III+	iv	V	VI	vii°	i
letter name:	Em	F♯°	G+	Am	B	C	D♯°	Em

Melodic minor scale

intervals:	P5 m3	P5 m3	aug5 M3	P5 M3	P5 M3	dim5 m3	dim5 m3	P5 m3
scale degree:	1	2	3	4	5	♯6	♯7	1
chord quality:	m	m	aug	M	M	dim	dim	m
Roman numeral:	i	ii	III+	IV	V	vi°	vii°	i
letter name:	Em	F♯m	G+	A	B	C♯°	D♯°	Em

So, to sum things up, triads are formed by stacking a 3rd and a 5th above each note of a major or minor scale. There are four types, or qualities, of triad: major, minor, diminished, and augmented. These four qualities result from different combinations of 3rds (major and minor) and 5ths (perfect, diminished, and augmented). This table summarizes the possible combinations:

	perfect 5th	diminished 5th	augmented 5th
major 3rd	major triad	*	augmented triad
minor 3rd	minor triad	diminished triad	**

* The combination of a major 3rd and a diminished 5th never occurs when making triads out of major and minor scales. There is no name for this triad (except "major triad with a lowered 5th").

** This combination also doesn't occur when making triads out of major and minor scales. It also happens to contain the same pitches as a different triad in first inversion, and so is usually named that way. You might occasionally see it named "minor triad with a raised fifth," written m(♯5) or m(+5).

Added and Altered Notes in Triads

Added Notes

There are also a couple of additions and alterations to the basic triads that we can cover here. The additions involve adding notes to the basic major and minor triads. These notes are the 2nd and the 6th. Here are the possible combinations with D major and D minor triads:

The "add2" chords are sometimes called "add9". They are also sometimes written without the word "add" (D2, A♭2, etc.). A "9" *without* the word "add" in front means something else, as we will see later in this chapter. If both the 2nd and the 6th are added, the chord is named "6/9" ("9" instead of "2" because of the way it is often spaced). It's also possible to have a minor 6/9.

Altered Notes

A common alteration of the major triad involves replacing the 3rd of the chord with a 4th. This is called a suspension. The term comes from classical music where most often the 4th is held over (suspended) from the previous chord. It's also possible to replace the 3rd with the 2nd, or even with both the 2nd *and* the 4th. Normally you will see this written with the abbreviation "sus," followed by either "2," "4," or both. If you see "sus" without any number after it, you can assume it means "sus4."

Four-note (7th) Chords

Although we created a few four-note chords by adding a 2nd or a 6th to a major or minor triad, most four-note chords are formed by adding a 7th to one of the four qualities of triads (major, minor, diminished, or augmented). The interval of a 7th comes in three useful sizes when it comes to forming chords: major, minor, and diminished. Let's review them quickly.

The major 7th is a half step less than an octave. The minor 7th is a whole step less than an octave. The diminished 7th contains the same pitches as a major 6th, and is often spelled as such for convenience, but technically should be spelled as a 7th.

Combining Triads with the Interval of a 7th

Now we can combine these three sizes of 7th with each of our four triads. That makes 12 possible combinations, although only five of them appear very commonly in gospel music. First, let's see how the combinations stack up; then we'll see where they appear in the major scale and in the various minor scales.

	major 7th	**minor 7th**	**diminished 7th**
major triad	major 7th chord	dominant 7th chord	*
minor triad	minor (maj7) chord	minor 7th chord	**
diminished triad	***	half-diminished 7th chord	fully-diminished 7th chord
augmented triad	major 7th (♯5)	dominant 7th (♯5)	****

*   This combination doesn't occur when forming 7th chords from major or minor scales. It has the same pitches as the major 6th chord discussed at the end of the previous section.

**   This combination doesn't occur when forming 7th chords from major or minor scales. It has the same pitches as the minor 6th chord discussed at the end of the previous section.

*** Although this combination doesn't occur when forming 7th chords from major or minor scales, it is sometimes considered an alteration/substitution for the fully-diminished 7th chord.

**** This combination doesn't occur when forming 7th chords from major or minor scales.

Now let's see where each of these occurs when forming 7th chords in each of the major and minor scales:

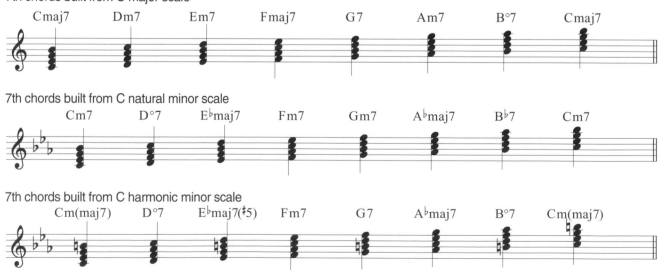

7th chords built from C major scale

7th chords built from C natural minor scale

7th chords built from C harmonic minor scale

7th chords built from C melodic minor scale

Note that when 7th chords are played on the piano they are often voiced so that the root is in the left hand and the remaining notes are in the right hand. The right-hand voicing forms its own triad with its "root" being the third of the main chord.

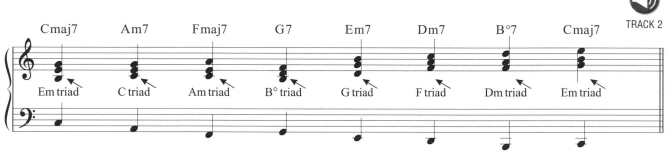

Chord Symbols

You may have noticed some unfamiliar symbols in the examples above. Perhaps this is a good time to talk about the abbreviations used in chord symbols. The most obvious abbreviations are "maj7" to mean a major 7th chord and "m7" to mean a minor 7th chord. You will sometimes see these abbreviated with symbols instead ("△7" means major 7th and "−7" means minor seventh). If you see only a "7" after the letter name of the chord (such as G7), this means it is a dominant 7th chord.

You may remember from earlier in this chapter that a small circle is the symbol for a diminished triad (for example, F♯°). Well, there are two types of diminished 7th chords: fully-diminished and half-diminished. The small circle combined with a "7" means a fully-diminished seventh chord (B°7). A small circle with a line through it combined with a "7" means a half-diminished seventh chord (Aø7). There are some who prefer the half-diminished 7th chord to be identified as a minor 7th chord with a lowered or flatted 5th. In that case you'll see it written like this: Am7(♭5). Either way, the pitches are the same.

You'll also see a chord in the above example labeled "maj7(♯5)"; and you might be confused because there is no sharp in front of any note in that chord. Well, in chord symbols the use of a ♯ or ♭ with a number really means "raised" or "lowered." You will find that the 5th of the chord in the example has been raised through the use of a natural sign, since the note had a flat originally. Sometimes you'll find that "+" and "−" are used to mean "raised" and "lowered" instead of ♯ or ♭. This makes some sense because we already use + for an augmented triad (in which the 5th is raised compared to a major or minor triad). But in order to avoid confusion, it's best not to use "−" as a symbol for minor at the same time; use "m" instead.

Here is a handy table of symbols and the most common abbreviations:

7th Chords	Common Abbreviations
major 7th	Cmaj7, C△7 (also sometimes CM7 or CMA7)
minor 7th	Cm7, C−7 (also sometimes Cmi7)
dominant 7th	C7
fully-diminished 7th	C°7
half-diminished 7th	Cø7, Cm7(♭5), Cm7(-5)
dominant 7th, raised 5th	C7(♯5), C7(+5), C+7
dominant 7th, lowered 5th	C7(♭5), C7(−5)
minor triad, major 7th	Cm(maj7), Cm(△7), Cm(+7)
major 7th, raised 5th	Cmaj7(♯5), Cmaj7(+5), C△7(♯5), C△7(+5)

Chords with Extensions

It's possible to have chords with five, six, and even seven notes. The additional notes (beyond the root, 3rd, 5th, and 7th we've discussed so far) are called extensions. They include the 9th, 11th, and 13th. They are pretty easy to see when the chord is stacked in root position:

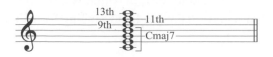

They may be somewhat harder to spot when the chord is spaced in a more "real world" way.

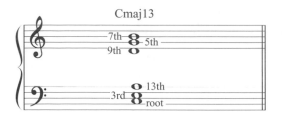

The Difference Between Extensions and Additions

At this point you might be asking yourself, "Aren't those really just the 2nd, 4th, and 6th? We already covered those!" Well, when those pitches are added to a *triad* they are, in fact, called the 2nd, 4th, and 6th. But when they are used with a *seventh chord* they are considered extensions rather than additions. In other words, if you see a chord designated as a 9, 11, or 13, you can be quite sure that it also contains a 7th.

Altered and Unaltered Extensions

Extensions are used to add color to a 7th chord. They can be added "as is" (unaltered compared to a major scale), but they can also be altered chromatically (by raising them or lowering them by a half step). When extensions are altered we identify the alteration in comparison to the major scale of the chord's root, not *in comparison to the key signature of the song we're playing in*. This is important. Here's an example that should make this clear. Let's take the chord C7♭9. Here it is in two different keys, F major and F minor:

Notice that in the first example (in F major) we need a ♭ in front of the note D (the 9th of C) in order to make it a ♭9. In the second example (in F minor), there is no accidental in front of D because the key signature already makes it flat. However, in both cases we still need to put a ♭ in the chord symbol, because the 9th is flat (or lowered) when compared to a C major scale.

Combining 7th Chords and Extensions

Obviously, if we can have up to seven notes in a chord, there are many possible combinations. Let's examine each type (or quality) of 7th chord individually to see which extensions work best.

Major 7th chord: The 9th and/or 13th can be added to a maj7 chord. The 9th is somewhat more common than the 13th. They should not be altered (no ♭9, ♯9, or ♭13). When the 13th is present, the 5th may be omitted to open up the voicing. Doing this doesn't change the quality of the chord.

The 11th is not used with a maj7 chord unless it is raised to ♯11 (the natural 11th conflicts with the major 3rd). The ♯11 is used mostly when the maj7 chord functions as the IV chord. When the ♯11 is used on a I chord it creates a very strong color that tends to "blur the tonality." Jazz musicians make frequent use of ♯11 on a I chord (especially on the final chord of a piece), but it isn't often used that way in gospel music.

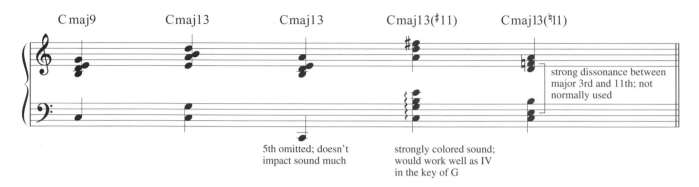

Note that each Cmaj13 chord also has a 9th, even though the chord symbol doesn't explicitly say so. It is always assumed that a maj13 chord *could* have a 9th as well.

Minor 7th chord: The 9th and/or 11th can be added to a m7 chord. The 9th is somewhat more common than the 11th. Neither should be altered. The 13th is seldom added to a m7 chord (in gospel music). As we discussed earlier in the chapter, it can be added to a minor triad to create a m6 or m6/9 chord:

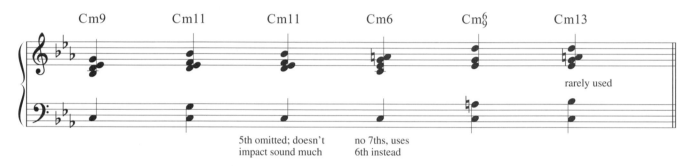

Note that each Cm11 chord also has a 9th, even though the chord symbol doesn't explicitly say so. It is always assumed that a m11 chord *could* have a 9th as well.

Dominant 7th chord: The dominant 7th chord has the most possibilities when it comes to adding and altering extensions. The 9th and/or 13th can be added to a dominant 7th chord; they are equally common. Each can be altered chromatically or left unaltered. The 9th can be altered by being raised or lowered by a half step. It's even possible to have *both* a lowered and a raised 9th at the same time. The 13th can be altered by lowering it a half step. The lowered 13th is the same pitch as the raised 5th, and will often be written as such in the chord symbol. Once again, the 5th (if unaltered) can usually be omitted to open up the sound without actually changing the quality of the chord. Here are some of the many possibilities with the 9th and 13th:

Note that the second C13 chord also has a 9th, even though the chord symbol doesn't explicitly say so. It is always assumed that a dom13 chord *could* have a 9th as well.

The 11th is dealt with in dominant 7th chords in a manner similar to that employed in maj7 chords. Since the 11th and the major 3rd conflict, the 11th, if present, is raised to ♯11, which is the same pitch as ♭5. If the natural 11th is used, then the major 3rd is omitted; this is essentially another way of writing "sus4."

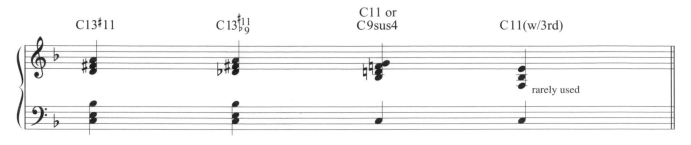

Note that the C13♯11 chord also has a 9th, even though the chord symbol doesn't explicitly say so. It is always assumed that a dom13 chord *could* have a 9th as well.

Half-diminished 7th chords: These chords handle extensions in a fashion similar to minor 7th chords. You can add the 9th and/or 11th. In contrast to the m7 chord, however, the 11th is a more common extension than the 9th. The 11th often substitutes for the minor 3rd. The 13th is not used.

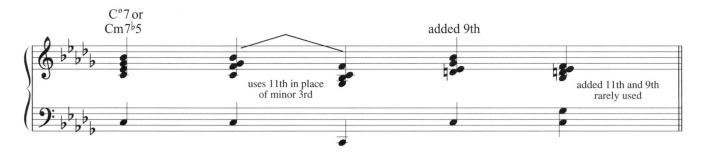

Note that unlike previous chords, the symbols for half-diminished chords usually don't spell out the extensions. Experienced players know that the 11th can be freely added, or alternatively the 9th could be, too.

Fully-diminished 7th chords: Because of their unique construction (basically a circle of minor thirds, any of which might be considered the root), fully-diminished seventh chords don't really use extensions in the same way as other 7th chords. In a way they are sort of like extensions themselves, because they form a dom7(♭9) chord without a root. Take a look:

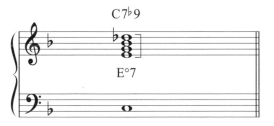

The one way that a fully-diminished 7th chord can be colored is by replacing one or two pitches with pitches a whole step higher. This works best when the substitute pitch(es) is/are still in the key signature.

Minor triad with major 7th chord: This chord can add both the 9th and the 13th. They should not be altered. An unaltered 11th is also possible, but less common.

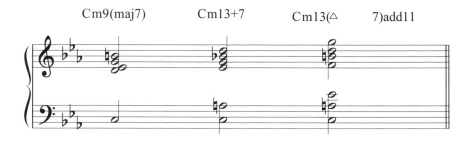

Note the three different ways to indicate that the 7th is raised (maj, +, and △).

Voicing Extensions as a Triad in the Right Hand

One last thing about seventh chords with extensions: Often the extensions can be arranged in the higher notes of the voicing to form a triad on their own (with a different root from the main chord). This is often an effective way to voice them; it also happens to be one of the common ways they find their way into gospel music. Here are a few examples:

Major 7th chords:

Minor 7th chords:

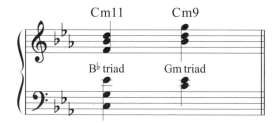

Dominant 7th chords:

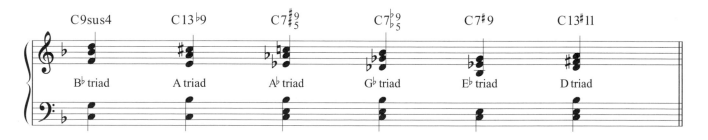

The first chord in the example above (C9sus4) is sometimes written Gm7/C. This is called a "slash chord," which brings us to the last section of this chapter.

Slash Chords

All of the chords we've discussed so far in this chapter are voiced with the root in the left hand (or bass). We can use "slash chords" to identify chords where some other part of the chord is in the bass. Here are some examples:

Simple triads and 7th chords:

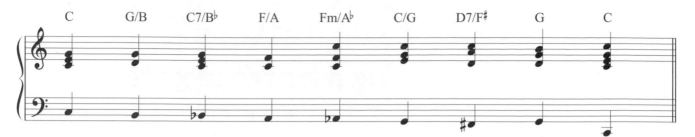

Slightly more complex:

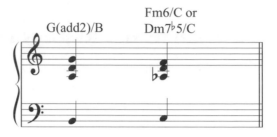

We can also use slash chords to identify a chord voicing that may be too cumbersome to write out in the standard way.

Lastly, we can use slash chords to indicate voicings that might be impossible to describe clearly with standard chord symbols.

I do need to caution you about a couple of aspects concerning the use of slash chords. First, don't use them when a standard chord symbol will suffice. This creates unnecessary confusion about the chord's function. (It also makes it harder for bass players to read, since they will always need to be looking at the lower part of the slash.) Secondly, when you do use slash chords, try not to mix sharps and flats between the two parts of the slash chord (i.e., notate as G♭/A♭, not F♯/A♭).

14

Chapter 2
HARMONIC DEVICES 1
STATIC SECTIONS IN MAJOR KEYS

One of the main responsibilities of the keyboardist in a gospel group is outlining the harmonic structure of the song. We also need to telegraph the harmony to the singer(s), and provide some interest in static sections. Let's take that last one first.

What do I mean by a static section? One in which the harmonic rhythm (the pace at which the chords change) is relatively slow. For instance, how do you make this interesting? It's just one chord for four measures!

In static sections, the goal is to create harmonic interest without actual chord progression. You'll notice that in all the upcoming examples we almost never play more than two or three chords without getting back to the original chord in some way. It's sort of like walking in a very small circle. We're moving, but we're not really going anyplace (on purpose!).

You'll also find that the right hand is almost always playing three-part harmony. This is because gospel harmony is fundamentally vocal, and the standard for most gospel choirs is three parts (soprano, alto, tenor) with bass notes either sung as a fourth part or, more commonly today, played instrumentally (by piano or bass). You will find that each part of the three-part harmony outlined in these examples is always easily sung and remembered.

In later chapters, we'll take what we've learned here and apply it to full-fledged chord progressions, and eventually to entire songs.

Backtracking (or Backcycling)

A simple but effective tool for static sections is called **backtracking**, which is a quick move to the IV chord and back again. It's accomplished by moving the 3rd and 5th of the I chord up **diatonically** (staying within the key signature) by step and back down again. Here's an example with an added bass line:

TRACK 3

Notice the "crushed" grace notes that are played by sliding the 2nd finger from the black key to the white key. These can be added throughout all of the examples in this book. They usually occur when sliding into the 3rd or 5th from a half step below.

Moving the Backtrack Chords

When the chords *do* change, the backtracking moves to the new chord and its own IV chord.

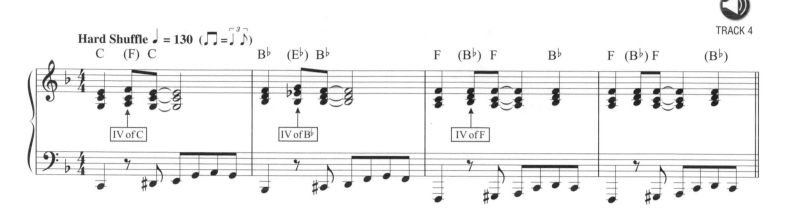

Extended Backtracking

It's also possible to extend the backtracking concept by using the IV of the IV. You may even try extending it back three levels:

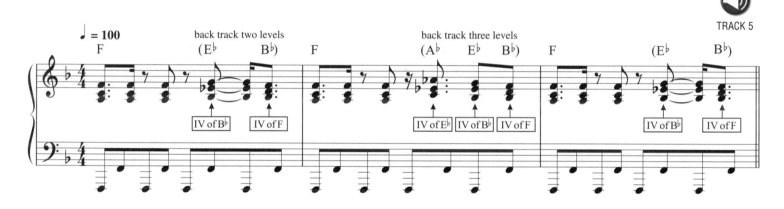

Backtracking Dominant 7th Chords

In a "bluesy" gospel song, the main chords are often dominant 7ths. You can backtrack these by moving the 3rd, 5th, and 7th up and back again (all three voices moving in parallel). This is shown in the first two bars of the next example. Keeping the 7th stationary can provide extra bite by creating an incomplete maj7 chord in the right hand. This is shown in measures 3–4 of the next example:

Rhythmic Variety

When backtracking, the IV chord usually ends up on beats 2 and/or 4, or on weaker beats that lead us back to the main chord on the downbeat. It's certainly possible to turn that around, however, and start the "back-track" chords on the downbeat. Here's an example with two levels of backtracking:

TRACK 7

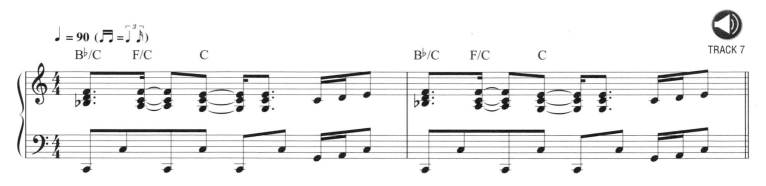

You can also augment the time scale of the backtracking. Here's an example (also with two levels of back-tracking) where each chord gets a full measure:

TRACK 8

Upper Neighbor Chords (the I–ii "Couple")

Similar to backtracking is the use of the upper neighbor chord. This is when all three notes of the main chord are moved up diatonically (staying within the key signature) by step. Here is a C major triad and its upper neighbor (in the key of C), the Dm triad:

TRACK 9a

One of the more useful things about this is that the combination of the main chord and its upper neighbor can harmonize six of the seven notes in a major scale. See how alternating the C major and Dm triads by moving through the inversions allows every note of the C major scale (except one: the 7th scale degree, also known as the leading tone—in the key of C it's the note B) to be the top melody note of the chord.

TRACK 9b

The harmonized six-note scale shown above is the key to understanding vocal harmony in gospel music. Many people think of gospel harmony as being based on the major pentatonic (five-note) scale, but in fact it's based on this six-note scale.

It's easy to see how the upper neighbor pair (sometimes called a "couple" by gospel players) can be applied to a static section. The right hand is made up entirely of C major and Dm triads in different inversions.

TRACK 10

Notice how this technique holds open many more possibilities for melodic as well as harmonic interest. We're not just going up and back, like we did with the backtracking examples, but moving through different inversions in the right hand. Also notice that this entire example is labeled with just one chord symbol, the C major chord. The Dm chords are a way of adding interest without leading the chord progression away from C major.

The I-ii° Couple

A technique that is often used, especially in ballads, is to borrow the ii chord from the parallel minor mode (from C minor, in this case). This is accomplished by making the upper neighbor to I a diminished triad instead of a minor triad. Here is a modified version of the previous example demonstrating this. The C major chords are all the same as in the previous example, but the Dm triads have all become D diminished triads by lowering the A to A♭.

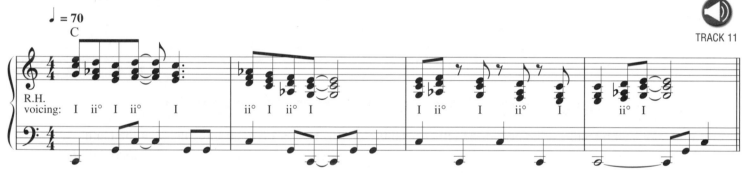

TRACK 11

"Trio" or Parallel Chords

Remember how we expanded on the concept of backtracking by backtracking two or even three levels? Well, it's also possible to expand the "couple" concept by using the "upper neighbor of the upper neighbor": in other words, the I chord, its upper neighbor (the ii chord), and the ii chord's upper neighbor (the iii chord). Perhaps we could call these a "trio." In the classical music world these are known as **parallel chords**. (More specifically, they are **diatonic** parallel chords, meaning that they move by the steps of the major or minor scale, in contrast to **chromatic** parallel chords, which move entirely by half steps.) There are four ways this is usually done in gospel music.

One is to stay completely within the key signature. The top chord of the trio (the iii chord) creates a major 7th chord against the root in the left hand (measures 2 and 4).

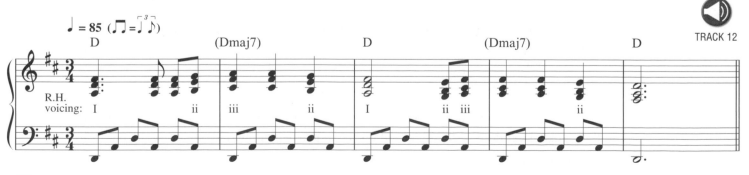

TRACK 12

Secondly, for a more "bluesy" sound, we can use a diminished iii chord to create a dominant 7th chord when combined with the root in the left hand. We do this by lowering the 7th scale degree (C#) to C♮ (measures 2 and 4).

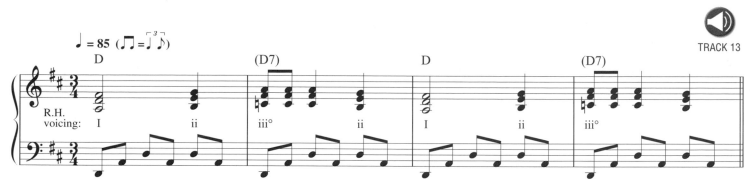

Thirdly, for an even more aggressively bluesy sound, we can lower both the 3rd and the 7th scale degrees. This creates an F major triad on the lowered 3rd scale degree, which combines with the root in the left hand to form a Dm7 chord (beat 1 of measures 2 and 4). Even this somewhat "crunchy" sound is still made up of three very singable parts.

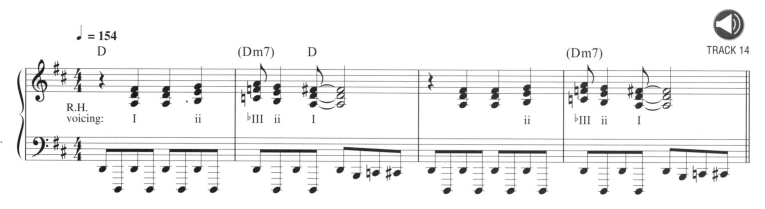

Lastly, we can make both of the upper neighbor chords (ii and iii) into diminished triads. This gives us the bluesy flavor of the dominant 7th that's created with the iii°, along with the wonderful ballad color of the ii°.

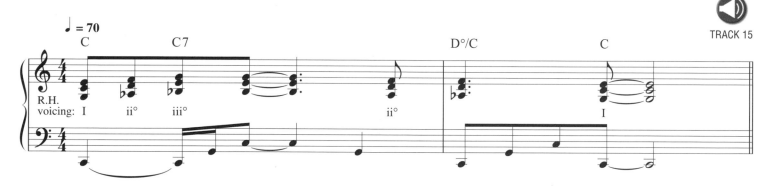

This device can also be stretched in time to great effect. Here we'll combine four chords—the I, the ii, the ii°, and the iii°—to create an entire eight-bar section that is essentially one long C chord. This example is in the style of "Faith" by Richard Smallwood & Vision:

Since both of the upper neighbor chords are of the same quality (in this case diminished triads), we can insert a passing chord between them that demonstrates the next device we'll discuss, **chromatic parallel chords** (chords of the same quality that move by half steps). You'll find it labeled as #ii° in measure 4, measure 8, and in the intro bar. Also notice how the bass line walks up chromatically at the end of measure 8 to propel us back to tonic.

Chromatic Parallel Chords

Chromatic parallel chords are similar to diatonic parallel chords, except that all of the notes move entirely by half steps (as in a chromatic scale) rather than by following the key signature. In gospel music these are used much more in the instrumental accompaniments than in the vocal harmonies. One notable exception is this "walk-up" figure:

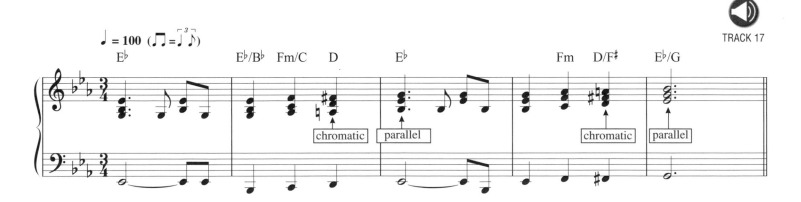

The Eb chord moves to its upper neighbor (Fm) and then is approached chromatically from below (D major to Eb major). This, like all the previous examples, is suitable for vocal harmony because all three parts outlined by the right hand are easily singable.

Since we are talking about static sections, we won't be moving too far from tonic. Three half steps is pretty much the extent to which we can move before it sounds as though we are leading the chord progression somewhere else. We can come back to tonic chromatically from above or below. This is more of an instrumental type of figure rather than a reflection of the vocal harmonies. Notice in the next example that the bass line follows the chromatic movement.

TRACK 18

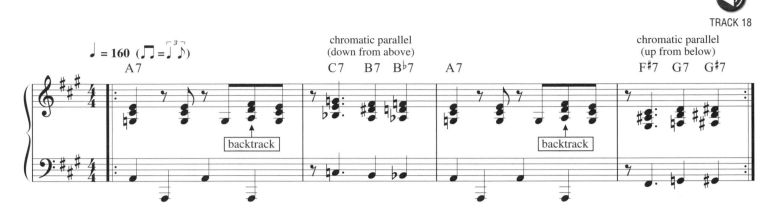

Here's another combination of backtracking and chromatic movement. Here the bass doesn't follow the chromatic movement; this results in C°7 chords in measures 3 and 4:

TRACK 19

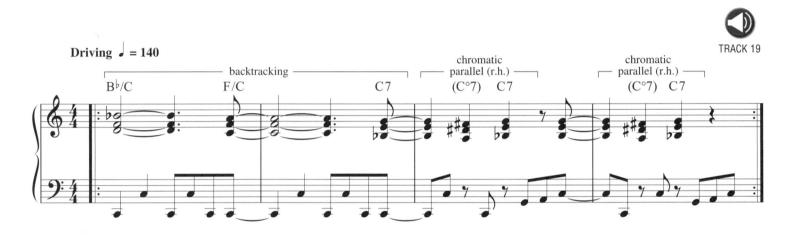

There's more to learn about both diatonic and chromatic parallelism, but it comes in the context of our next chapters, where we learn to apply these concepts in larger-scale chord progressions.

Chapter 3
HARMONIC DEVICES 2
EXPANDING ON THE "COUPLE" CONCEPT

Now that we've practiced using backtracking, upper-neighbor "couples," diatonic parallel chords ("triples"), and chromatic parallel chords to elaborate one basic chord, we're going to learn to connect chords into progressions using one of these devices. Let's go back to our basic "couple," the major triad (I) and its upper neighbor, either the minor triad (ii) or the diminished triad (ii°).

Combining "Couples" with Various Bass Notes to Create Complete Chords

Simple Combinations

We can create new complete chords by combining the lower chord of the couple (I) with other bass notes. Let's take a look at the possibilities in C major. The simplest choice is to play the C major triad with either the 3rd or the 5th in the bass.

It's also pretty easy to see how the C triad can be combined with A in the bass to form an Am7 chord.

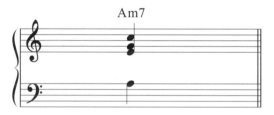

We can do the same things with the ii chord, Dm. First, let's use the 3rd and the 5th as bass notes.

In the same way we turned the C major triad into an Am7 chord, we can turn the D minor triad into a Bm7♭5 (also written B⌀7, meaning B half-diminished) by adding B in the bass.

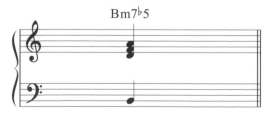

The Dm triad with G in the bass can stand on its own as Dm/G, but it can also imply one of three different, more complete chords.

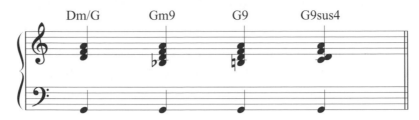

Just using the examples we've looked at so far, we can create a short musical phrase that goes through a full chord progression.

TRACK 20

All of the right-hand voicings are either a I chord or a ii chord (except for the F/A and G/B at the end that bring us back to C). Even so, our ears tell us we've heard a complete progression. In fact, our ears tell us that we basically heard this (which looks like it could come from a pop or country chart):

So then why does the written-out version sound like gospel? It's the sound of the alternating I and ii chords in the right hand (the "couples"), the linear movement in the bass, and the anticipated syncopations that give it that characteristic gospel sound.

Using the I Chord over IV or ii in the Bass

Here's another example with a couple of new twists (beside the fact that it's in the key of D):

TRACK 21

Did you spot the two new chords? The first one is the D/G in measures 3–4. The bass note goes to IV, but we've harmonized it with the I chord instead of the ii chord that we used previously. The result is something that sounds a lot like a Gmaj9 (but with no 3rd). It's a nice open sound that retains the three-part harmony so characteristic of gospel music, yet gives the illusion of a thicker five-note chord.

The other new chord happens for just a moment. It's the D/E in measure 7. In this context it works as a **suspension** (consisting of non-chord tones carried over—suspended—from the previous chord in measure 6 and resolved later, to the Em triad on beat 2).

The D/E chord could also be used as an independent chord (not a passing chord or a suspension) in two possible ways. One is as a V chord leading to A (it might also be notated as E9sus4 in that case), and the other is as an incomplete Em11 chord.

Combining the Diminished Triad with Other Bass Notes

I think we're ready to start adding the ii° triad for some color. Here's an example in A♭ that uses both the ii minor chord (B♭m) and the ii° (B♭°) in the right hand. Notice how the ii° opens up possibilities for different bass lines as well.

Besides adding the ii° triad in measures 4–6, we also sneaked in a couple of new right-hand/bass-note combinations. In measure 2 we have the I chord along with the flatted 7th scale degree in the bass (A♭/G♭). This really pushes the bass line down to the next note, F. Also, in measure 6 we have a G♭7 (♭VII7) resulting from the combination of that same flatted 7th in the bass with the ii° triad in the right hand.

By the way, in addition to the I chord and the ii° chord, the ii minor chord can also combine with the flatted 7th scale degree. It creates a maj7 chord (♭VIImaj7). Here's a quick example in F:

Not only did we use the ♭VIImaj7 chord in measure 3, but we also brought back the "trio" (two levels of upper neighbor from the previous chapter) in measure 1.

Adding Notes to the Diminished Triad

OK, let's get back to the subject of this section, the ii° chord. The diminished triad can be a part of so many chords that it's easy to get lost in all the possibilities! As we've already seen, it can be used without any added notes in root position and two inversions. Here they are with a D diminished triad:

By adding a B♮ to our D diminished triad we end up with a B fully-diminished 7th chord (B°7), allowing for four possible versions. Because of the symmetrical way in which such chords are built (all intervals are minor thirds), we can also rename each inversion as a root position chord. You will notice that renamed chords are spelled to make them easier to read, even if the spellings aren't technically correct. (For instance, the A♭°7 chord should really be spelled A♭–C♭–E♭♭–G♭♭, but would you really want to read that?)

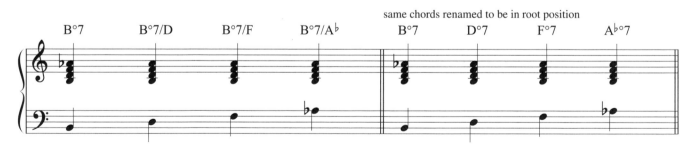

Although it's not in the C major scale, a B♭ can be added in the bass to create a B♭7 chord. (This is the ♭VII7 we discussed earlier in this section.)

We can also add a C to our D diminished triad. We end up with a chord that could be named either D half-diminished 7th (written as Dm7♭5) or Fm6, depending on the context. Being a four-note chord, it also has four versions.

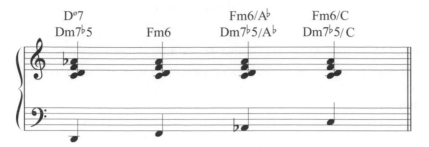

By using G as our bass note along with the D diminished triad, we can imply two possible chords. The first one is pretty straightforward: it's a G7♭9. We just have to add a B♮ to complete the voicing. The second one is easier to play than it is to name! It's simply the chord taken from the example above and placed over a G in the bass. I would probably name it Fm6/G or Dm7♭5/G. (Sometimes, especially when notating a bass chart, I might opt for G7♭9(sus4). Why? Because gospel music contains so many slash chords and bass players are primarily interested in the second half of a slash chord. A whole string of slash chords can make a bass chart unnecessarily difficult to read by forcing the bass player to search for the note after each slash.)

The G7♭9 is formed by making our basic diminished triad into a fully-diminished 7th chord (by adding B), then placing the G in the bass. That same fully-diminished 7th chord can be a part of three other dominant7(♭9) chords.

I'll give the same disclaimer here, that these chords are not spelled correctly from a purely theoretical standpoint. Instead, they are spelled to be easiest to read and to help you make the connection that they are all the same chord in the right hand. Only the bass note is changing for each new chord.

How about some musical examples to help all of this sink in...?

Here's an example in the key of G where all of the ii chords are diminished. In the course of this short example, the ii° chord is combined with *eight* different bass notes to create *nine* different chords.

This example really exploits the use of the diminished triad as part of a dominant 7th and/or dom7♭9 chord. It's part of the D7♭9 in measure 1, the F7 in measure 2, and the B7♭9 in measure 3. It also forms the upper notes of F♯°7 in measure 3. In the rest of the example it is simply A° or Am7♭5 with various bass notes.

Harmonizing the 7th Scale Degree (Leading Tone)
Using V, V7, or vii°

You may have also noticed one of the major limitations of using only "couple" chords (I and ii): there's no way to harmonize the 7th scale degree (also known as the **leading tone**, because of the way it *leads* back to the tonic). So, how do you harmonize the leading tone in gospel music? Since we're still working with three-part harmony and a preference for parallel motion in the right hand, these harmonies are what you'll find most of the time.

The first voicing is simple enough, just a straightforward V–I. Keep in mind, however, that if this harmony were sung by a gospel choir, rather than played by a keyboardist, the altos would have to remember to stay on their note (G) instead of moving in parallel with the melody. That's why a choir may just as often choose the second example with all the voices moving in parallel, in effect a *lower* neighbor. I've included the last version (B°–C) because it makes the point that parallel octaves aren't frowned upon in gospel music the way they are in traditional classical music theory. (If you have any amount of classical theory training, I'm sure this last example made you cringe!)

Here's an example that brings back the "trio" movement in measure 1. In measure 4 it harmonizes the leading tone with V7 by using V in the bass and vii° in the right hand.

Also note how the top "trio" chord (iii°) combines with E♮ in the bass to form an E♭7 in measure 3, which pulls us strongly to the Fm chord. An easy way to create a strong (but temporary) pull to a chord other than I is to precede it either by its own V7 (called a **secondary dominant chord**) or by its own vii°7/vii(m7♭5) chord (called a **secondary leading-tone** chord). In this case the chord toward which we are trying to pull is Fm. We achieve that by preceding it by its own V7 (secondary dominant: C7) or by its own vii°7 (secondary leading tone: E°7). We'll return to secondary dominants and secondary leading tones in Chapter 4.

Using iii7

Here's an example where the leading tone is harmonized with a iii7 chord (Fm7 in this case: iii7 in the key of D♭). The right-hand voicing is V–I, but the bass notes obviously make the full chord progression iii7 (Fm7) to vi7 (B♭m7). A little backtracking is brought in for measures 5–6 to resolve the chord progression back to I.

This next example is in the style of "Thank God for the Blood" by the Florida Mass Choir. The leading tone pops up twice, first harmonized by iii7 (Bm7 in measure 5) and then V (D chord in measure 6). Also take note of the way the figure in the first three bars is harmonized differently each time it's played ("couple," "trio," and altered "trio"). Going from G to Gmaj7 to G7 (which is the secondary dominant of C) really helps push toward the Cmaj9 chord (as does substituting a D♭ on the last beat of measure 3—a technique called **tritone substitution**, which we will cover in Chapter 4).

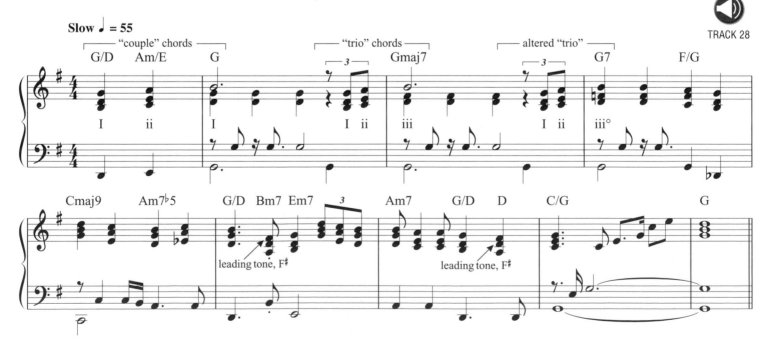

Here's a more up-tempo example in the style of "Just As I Am" by the Chicago Mass Choir. You'll find many of the things we've already talked about, plus a few more.

In the first 2 beats (the pickup measure), there are those parallel octaves between the bass and the melody. In the first full measure you'll find the chord E♭/D♭. As we saw previously, using a major triad with its own ♭7 in the bass produces a strong downward push on the bass line (down to A♭/C in this case). In measure 4 we have another example of a secondary leading tone chord, A°7 leading to B♭m. You may also notice the blatant parallel octaves in measure 3 (going from E♭/G to A♭).

Measures 5–8 are nearly the same as measures 1–4. Rhythmically, however, the roles of the right and left hands are reversed. In measure 1 the right hand is "on beat" while the left hand plays more "off beat." In measure 5 the right hand is now "off beat," so the left hand plays "on beat." Also, in measure 6 the bass line changes slightly. The note F is brought in to create an Fm7—a small change to add some variety, but it doesn't impact the upper harmony in the right hand. This means that a choir wouldn't have to remember to change harmonies there.

One fine point about having a choir sing these harmonies: In the second measure we have ii° (B♭°) followed by a ii minor (B♭m) with no other chord in between. If the right-hand voicing didn't change inversions it would force the altos to make a chromatic move while all the other voices stayed on the same note. Not good. The inversion change helps avoid the whole issue.

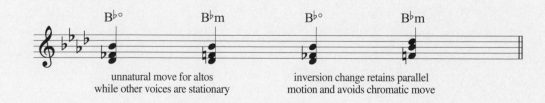

unnatural move for altos
while other voices are stationary

inversion change retains parallel
motion and avoids chromatic move

About this time you may be asking yourself, "Certainly gospel music doesn't just consist of 'couple' and 'trio' chords over a bass line, with V or iii thrown in if the melody happens to use the leading tone, and an occasional bit of backtracking for spice… does it?" Of course not! But this method of harmonization (or at least the extensive use of it) is unique to gospel music and it's an essential foundation for the upcoming chapters. That's why we're spending a fair amount of time on it. It truly is a system of harmony in its own right.

In the next chapter we'll move the "couple" to the 5th scale degree (V–vi, instead of I–ii) and the 4th scale degree (IV–v), and start looking at more uses of secondary dominants and secondary leading tones. We'll also explore some of those great "altered chords" that give gospel harmony such a funky sound.

Chapter 4

HARMONIC DEVICES 3
MOVING THE "COUPLE" (PLUS MORE SECONDARY CHORDS AND ALTERED CHORDS)

We've developed a pretty good idea of how the "couple" pair works on the 1st and 2nd scale degrees (I–ii or I–ii°). There's one other place in a major key where we have a major triad whose upper neighbor is a minor triad (V and vi).

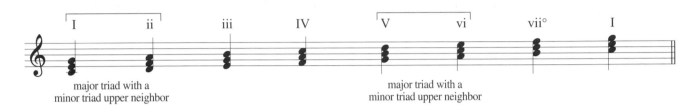

This really opens up the possibilities when creating gospel harmonies. Part of the art of writing and playing gospel is in the seamless transitions between couple pairs.

Moving the "Couple" to V and vi

Here's an example of the "couple" switching from I–ii to V–vi. We're in the key of F, so the I–ii pair is F–Gm and the V–vi pair is C–Dm. The first three bars use I–ii. In measure 4 we have a secondary dominant (remember those from last chapter?) that leads us to Dm. Since Dm is vi in the key of F, it's easy to see how the harmonization switches to V–vi. We also have a lower neighbor to C (B°) helping to create the G7 chord (secondary dominant leading us to C) in measure 6. In measures 7–8 we bring back the I–ii "couple" so we can transition back to an F chord. This one is in the style of "Wash Me Lord" by John P. Kee.

TRACK 30

This next example uses the V–vi "couple" in very much the same way.

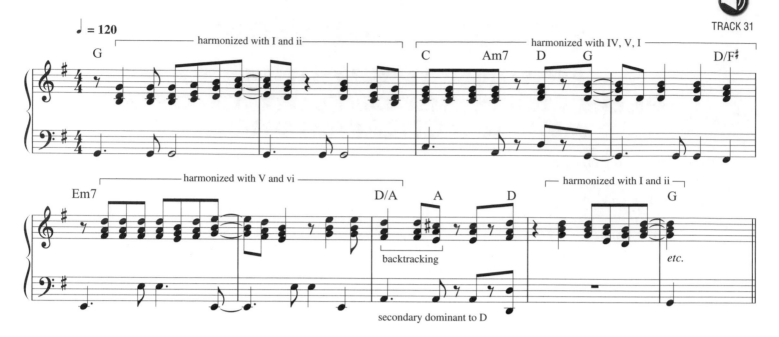

Measures 1–2 use the I–ii "couple." Measures 3–4 use a standard IV–V–I that could be found in almost any other music, be it pop or classical or country. In measures 5–6 we find the vi7 chord (Em7) harmonized with the V–vi "couple." In measure 7 the V chord becomes part of a quick backtracking pair with the A chord. Also, being an A major chord (rather than the A minor that would normally be found in the key of G) makes it a secondary dominant to the D, which then leads back to the tonic, G major.

Here's a short example in the style of "Suddenly" by Bishop Eddie Long and the New Birth Total Praise Choir. It's in A♭, which means our I–ii "couple" is A♭–B♭m. But this excerpt starts with a "couple" of E♭–Fm, V–vi in the key of A♭. It's not until measure 7 that we get to I–ii.

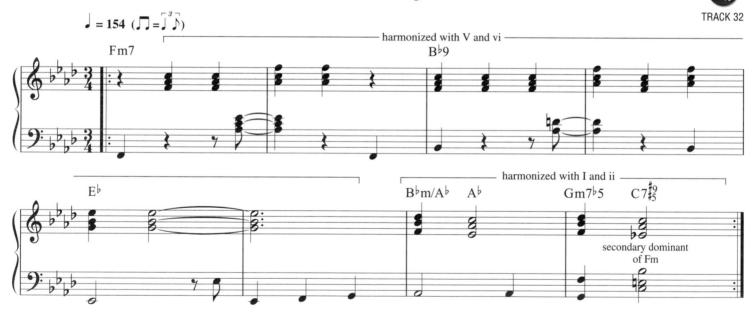

The last chord in that example is our first glimpse of an altered chord (C7♯5♯9). It comes about because the chord progression needs to get back to Fm. The secondary dominant of Fm is C7, but we have a problem because the choir still wants to sing its A♭ major triad, repeating the prior bar. But is this really a problem? No, we just do both! The right hand (or the choir) sounds an A♭ major triad while the left hand simultaneously plays a C7. Whether this technique came about because of a happy accident or sophisticated arranging doesn't matter; it sounds great! (You might notice that the C7 chord in the left hand has no 5th. This is because it would conflict with the A♭ in the right hand, which is functioning as ♯5, enharmonically the same as G♯.)

Here's a further altered version that could be used on the repeat. The I chord that was in measure 7 has been turned into an altered chord by keeping the A♭ triad in the right hand but using a D♮ in the bass to create an altered D7 chord (D7♭5♭9). (This one's really crunchy!) D7 is the secondary dominant to G. This creates root movement of a **circle of fifths** leading back to Fm (D⟶G⟶C⟶F).

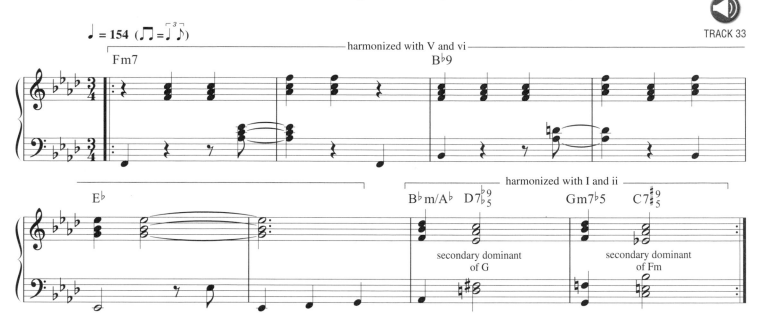

Moving the "Couple" to IV and v

Another place we sometimes get a "couple" is on the 4th scale degree. Since our "couples" are a combination of a major triad main chord and a minor or diminished triad as the upper neighbor, how do we get this on the 4th scale degree? The upper neighbor to IV is V, and that's another major triad. The answer is that we have to alter the V triad temporarily, making it minor.

Here's an example in the style of "Every Day Is Thanksgiving" by Leonard Burks. It starts out with the I–ii "couple." In the second measure it switches to IV–v and creates a secondary leading tone to B♭. We return to the I-ii couple; then there's a secondary dominant (G7) that leads us to the C in measures 5–6. The "trio" chords to the C chord are both diminished triads (D° and E°), with a chromatic passing chord (D♯°) between them. The E° triad with C in the bass forms a C7 chord. For the last two measures we're back to the I–ii pair.

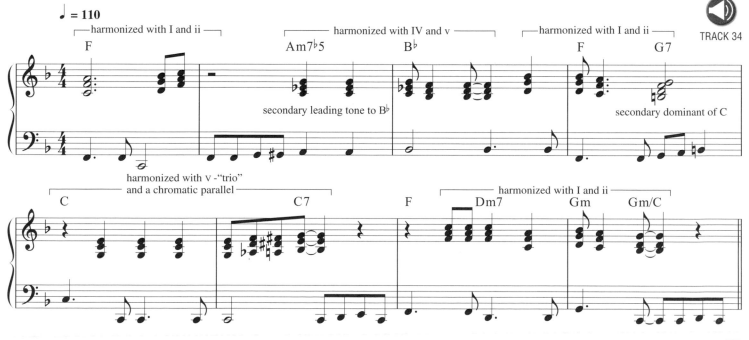

More on Secondary Chords

Gospel music makes frequent use of secondary dominant and secondary leading-tone chords to dress up chord progressions. They create a stronger pull to each new chord.

Simple Secondary Dominants

Here's an up-tempo shuffle groove in A♭ that just alternates between I and IV. It uses the backtracking technique we learned previously.

TRACK 35a

Now we'll make the fourth measure have a stronger pull back to tonic by using the dominant V7 (E♭7) and its secondary dominant (B♭7).

TRACK 35b

We've also altered the E♭7 slightly by using a ♭9 (F♭) to create a chromatic motion in the right hand.

Adding the Secondary Leading Tone

Here's a simple chord progression in B♭:

Now let's place a secondary dominant or secondary leading tone in front of each new chord.

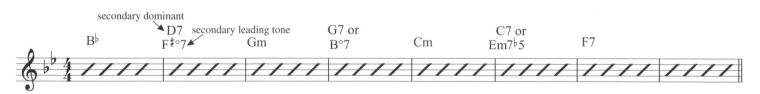

You might notice that in the above example the first two secondary leading-tone chords are fully-diminished 7th chords (F♯°7 and B°7), but the third one (Em7♭5) is half-diminished. Usually, when moving to a minor chord, it sounds best to use a fully-diminished secondary leading-tone chord. When moving to a major chord, you can use either a fully-diminished or a half-diminished secondary leading-tone chord, but half-diminished is more common.

Using everything we've learned up to this point, let's see how the chord progression from the previous example might actually be played.

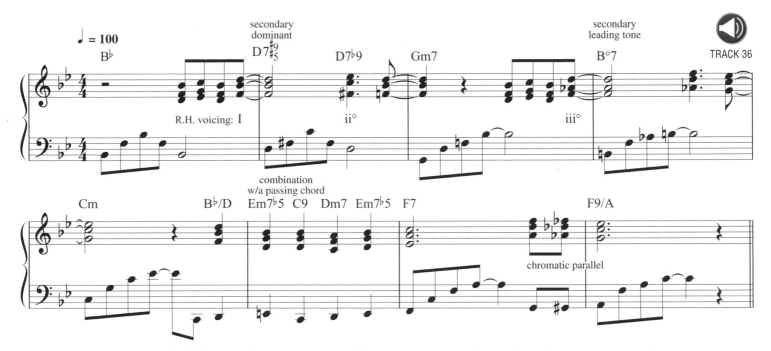

In measure 2 the I–ii° "couple" in the right hand is played over the D7 in the left hand to create altered dominant 7th chords. In measure 4 the top "trio" chord (iii°) is combined with B♮ to create the B°7. In measure 6 the right hand moves to the V–vi "couple" and we add E♮ in the bass to create the secondary movement to F7.

As a little aside, let's take a quick look at measures 7–8 in the previous example. It's a figure common in gospel music that uses parallel chromatic chords. It creates interest when the chord progression lands on a dominant 7th chord. It's based on the fact that both ii and iii are minor triads that can be played over V7 to create more colorful chords.

Let's look at it in the key of C:

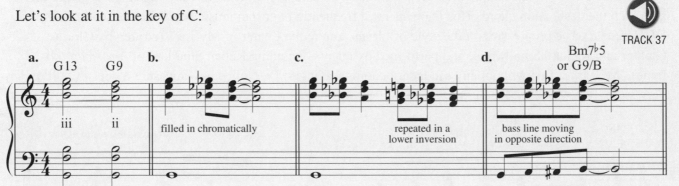

Example a. shows how the iii and ii chords combine with G7 to make G13 and G9 chords. Example b. adds a chromatic passing chord between iii and ii. This works because both ii and iii are of the same chord quality (both are minor triads). In Example c. the figure is repeated in a lower inversion to lengthen it. Notice how this results in a complete chromatic scale in the melody from G down to D. The bass line ascends in **contrary motion** (in the opposite direction of the melody) in Example d. (This figure works well with dominant 7th chords, including secondary dominants—as long as they aren't altered, i.e., ♯9, ♭5, etc.)

Delayed Resolution

This next example uses a couple of secondary dominants. The first one, at the end of measure 4, uses ii° in the right hand with G♯ in the bass to create a secondary dominant to C♯m7(vi7). In measure 6 the right hand switches to the V–vi "couple." This helps produce an F♯9 chord, a secondary dominant to B. (During the F♯9 we once again find the chromatic figure discussed in the last paragraph.) Instead of going directly to B, we go to F♯m7 which delays the resolution to B until the middle of the next measure.

Secondary ii7–V7

Another very common technique involving secondary dominants is to use both a ii7 and a V7 together to approach the destination chord. This happens most frequently in gospel music when the destination chord is IV. Here is a basic progression in the style of "Jesus, You're the Center of My Joy" (written by Gloria Gaither and Richard Smallwood, and performed by many—including Ruben Studdard of *American Idol* fame). We'll try it first without any secondary chords leading to IV. Notice how measure 2 doesn't pull us very strongly towards the IV chord.

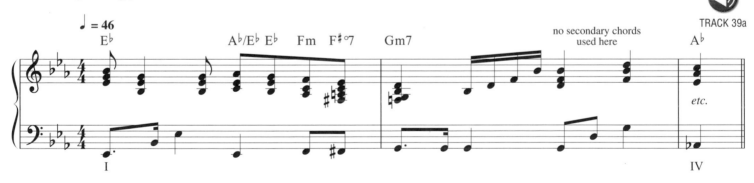

Now let's put a secondary ii7–V7 pair in front of the A♭ triad. In other words, we'll precede the A♭ with its own ii7 (B♭m7) and V7 (E♭7). You'll hear how much more convincing this chord progression sounds now.

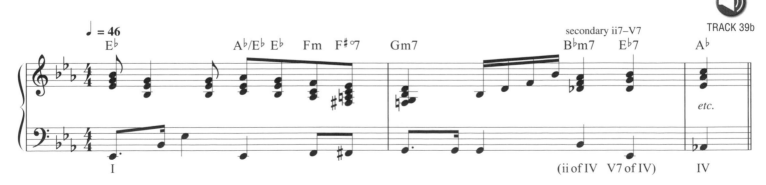

36

Altered Chords

One of the other characteristics of gospel harmony is the use of altered chords. We've encountered a few of them already. Consider, for instance, that all of the following chords have a C major triad in the right hand.

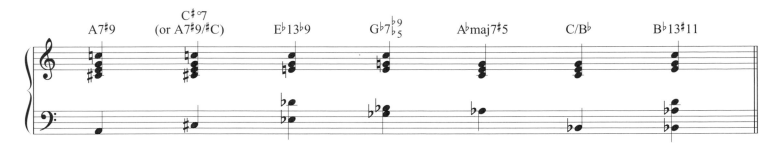

Some of these sound pretty crunchy when they are played individually and out of context, but any of them might be found in gospel music.

Dominant 7th(♯9)

Here's a typical gospel shuffle that uses the first two chords in the lineup above. Listen to what a great, funky sound the A7♯9 chord gives to this simple chord progression. Even when the bass moves up to C♯, the dissonance still seems natural. (If this were arranged for a choir, they would sing the top three notes of the right hand. If you play each voice individually, you'll hear that all three parts are easily heard and totally singable.)

TRACK 40

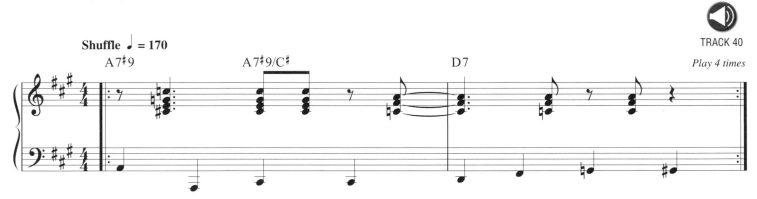

Fully-Diminished 7th with Raised Notes

The voicing that is named A7♯9/C♯ in the above example can also be used as an extended version of a fully-diminished 7th chord (C♯°7). Here's an example in the key of D major in the style of "It's Mighty Nice (To Be on the Lord's Side)" by Rev. Ernest Davis Jr.'s Wilmington-Chester Mass Choir. The chord to listen for is the A♯°7 in measure 4.

TRACK 41

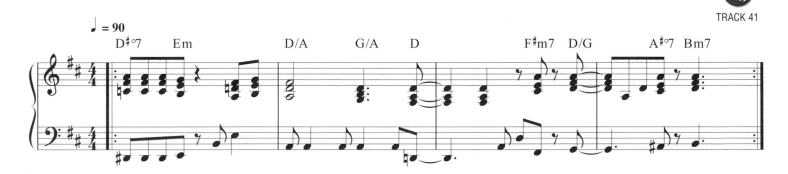

You'll notice that the top note in the A♯°7 is an A♮ instead of the usual G. That's why I referred to it as an *extended* fully-diminished 7th chord.

This technique of extending a fully-diminished 7th chord is borrowed from jazz voicing. Jazz players like to color the sound of this chord by raising one or two of its notes by a whole step, as long as the raised note(s) are still in the key signature (or whatever key they are currently in). Here's a quick example to show how it works:

TRACK 42

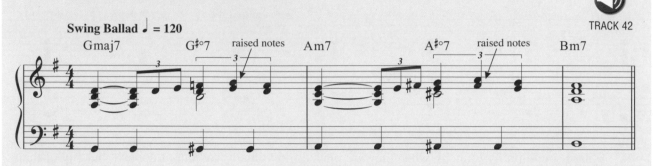

The middle notes of each quarter-note triplet are a whole step higher than the notes on either side of them (which are the actual chord tones). It works because those raised notes are still in the key of G (even if the notes they are raised *from* are not).

Tritone Substitution

Another altered chord that gospel players use to create more colorful progressions is the **tritone substitution**. In its simplest version you just replace the bass note of a root position dominant 7th chord by a note that is three whole steps (also known as a tritone) away. (Since a tritone is exactly half an octave it doesn't matter if you go up or down three whole steps, you will end up on the same pitch either way.) Dominant 7th chords usually resolve down a perfect 5th; this device moves the bass note to one half step above its next destination. Here it is in C major:

TRACK 43

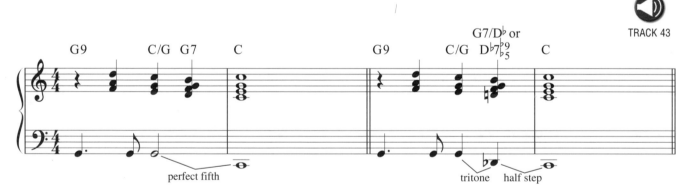

You may also want to consider flatting the 5th of the dominant 7th chord so that it isn't quite as dissonant with the bass (but only if altering it doesn't interfere with the melody or vocal harmonies!).

TRACK 44

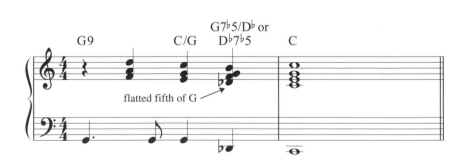

Why does the tritone substitution work? To understand this, you first need to know that:

a. Tritone substitutions are generally used only on dominant 7th chords. ("Jazzers" will know that a ii–V pair can also be substituted in this manner, but that is more of a jazz device than a gospel one.)

b. The main identifying notes in a dominant 7th chord are the 3rd and the 7th (they are what makes a dominant 7th sound different from a maj7 or a min7).

c. The 3rd and 7th have a strong pull toward the tonic chord.

The 3rd and 7th of a dominant 7th have a strong pull to the tonic chord because they resolve in opposite directions, each one by half step. There is another dom7 chord that shares the same two important notes. Its root is a tritone away, its 3rd is the former 7th, and its 7th is the former 3rd; it resolves to the tonic just as strongly.

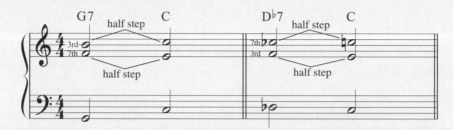

The goal of both progressions is the same (the tonic C triad). In the first progression, this goal is preceded by its dominant 7th (G7), while the second progression features a substitute for G7 (D♭7, a tritone away). Only the bass differs; in both progressions, the right-hand dyads are the same: F–B/C♭ moving to E–C.

Let's go back to "Jesus, You're the Center of My Joy." We saw earlier how to use a secondary ii7–V7 pair to lead to the IV chord. Here we'll take it a step further and use a tritone substitution on the secondary V7 (A7 in place of E♭7). In measure 2 we use only the substitute chord, which creates a nice chromatic movement in the bass. In measure 5 we'll use the original E♭7, then go to A7. This gives the more surprising effect of a tritone leap in the bass.

TRACK 45

The add2 Chord

Although it's not technically an altered chord in the sense that any notes in the chord have been raised or lowered, the add2 chord (sometimes called add9) is one that pops up more and more in modern pop/gospel music. It brings some color to a major or minor triad by adding a major 2nd above the root.

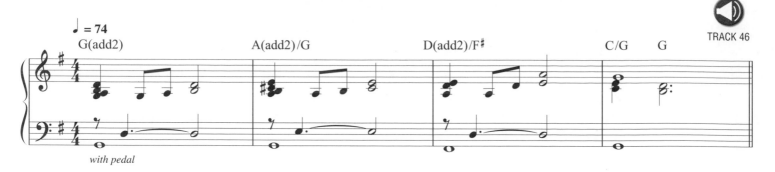

TRACK 46

with pedal

This next example treats the added 2nd more like a suspension that needs to resolve to the root before the arrival of the next chord.

TRACK 47

In measures 7–8 in the above example, you also find the add2 chord with the third in the bass. Usually the third is then left out of the right-hand voicing, creating a more open sound. This is because the right-hand voicing is now made up of 2nds, 4ths, and 5ths, instead of stacked 3rds. It's quite a texture change, and as such is used mainly in instrumental parts; only on rare occasions would a choir sing such a voicing.

Here's a more extensive use of the add2 with the third in the bass. It's based on the introduction to "It's Mighty Nice," a song we referenced earlier. Note that sometimes the word "add" is omitted from the chord symbol.

TRACK 48

Dominant 7th (♯5)

The last of the most common altered chords in gospel music is the dominant 7th with a raised 5th. It comes up fairly regularly in minor keys.

TRACK 49

Dominant 7th (♯5, ♯9)

The dominant 7th (♯5) is also used frequently with both a ♯5 and a ♯9. This is the device we encountered earlier, in which the choir (right-hand voicing) stays on its notes (the I chord) while the band (left hand) plays a secondary dominant to move to vi. Play them both and you get the dom7(♯5♯9) chord (measure 2 in the next example).

TRACK 50

Since the subject of minor keys has now come up, let's deal with it in the next chapter.

Chapter 5

HARMONIC DEVICES 4
MINOR KEYS

Everything we've covered up to this point has been based on the assumption that the song we're playing is in a major key. Of course, that's not always the case in the real world! It's just that the concepts we've covered so far are easier to grasp without throwing in some of the variables that crop up in minor keys. But now I think we're ready to apply what we've learned to minor keys.

Minor-key "couples" and "trios"
Minor "couple" using i and VII

Since our original "couple" pairing used a major triad and a minor triad to harmonize six out of the seven notes of the major scale, why can't we use the same pairing in a minor key? We can! The difference is that now the minor chord is tonic (i) and the major chord is VII.

Here's an example using this couple pairing in the key of C minor. The i chord is obviously Cm and the VII chord is B♭:

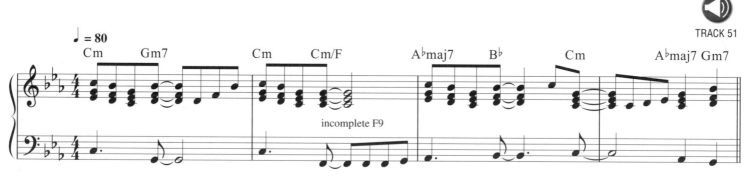

This couple implies the natural minor scale because it uses B♭ instead of the leading tone B♮. This leaves us with a minor v7 chord (Gm7) and no dominant 7th chords at all. The closest we get is the incomplete F9 in measure 2. We could leave this basic three-part harmony intact and fill out the missing notes.

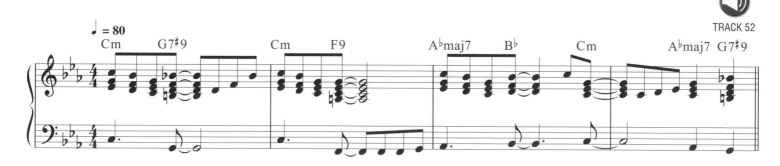

Filling out the voicing gets the leading tone (B♮) and raised 6th scale degree (A♮) into the inner parts, but still doesn't give us a way to harmonize a leading tone in the melody. For that we need our next device.

Minor "Trio" Using i with ii° and vii°

We simply combine the tonic minor chord with its upper neighbor (ii°) and its lower neighbor (vii°, built from the leading tone). (Sort of a "trio," but instead of two upper neighbors as we had before, this is an upper neighbor and a lower neighbor.) This allows us to harmonize every note of the harmonic minor scale, some of them with more than one triad.

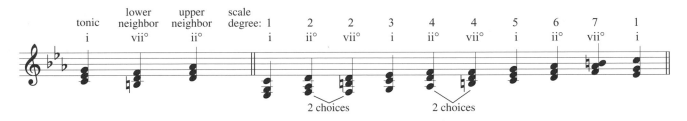

The next example shows this technique in action. It starts in C minor. In measure 4 it uses a secondary dominant (D7) to modulate to G minor, then comes back to C minor.

TRACK 53

As always, the way to check this example for real-world use is to try to sing each of the three parts outlined in the right hand. I think you'll find that all of them are pretty singable, even with the two modulations. The real trick in minor keys is to avoid making one of the parts sing the augmented 2nd interval between the 6th scale degree and the leading tone (A♭ and B♮ in this case). In the example above no voice has to sing those two notes back-to-back.

Minor "Couple" Using III and iv (Borrowed from Relative Major)

An additional "couple" that can be used in a minor key is the I–ii pair borrowed from the relative major key. For example, if we are in the key of A minor, then the relative major key is C major. The I–ii pair is our old friends C and Dm, but they are III–iv in the key of A minor.

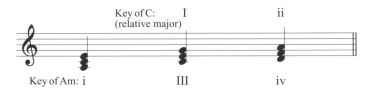

43

This example shows how this couple can be used in a chord progression that's definitely in the key of A minor (*not* C major).

TRACK 54

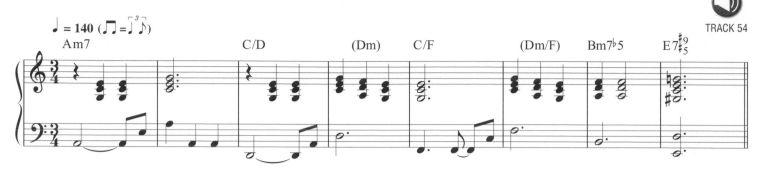

Combining These Methods

This next example combines all three of the minor-key techniques we've talked about so far. It's in the style of "We Made It (We Survived)" by Hezekiah Walker and the Love Fellowship Choir. (I've left this example in the somewhat challenging key of E♭ minor, since that is the key the real song is in.) In the lead-up measure and through the first three and a half full measures, you'll find a mix of i-vii° (E♭m–D°) and i–VII (E♭m–D♭): basically tonic and its two possible lower neighbors. Starting with the E♭m7 chord in the fourth full measure, the right hand switches to the relative-major "couple" (G♭–A♭m). The G♭ triad is filled out to make the altered V7 chord (B♭7♯5♯9) in measures 6 and 8. Starting with the B°7 in measure 8, the right hand goes back to i with both upper and lower neighbors (F° and D°). The last two chords use the relative-major pair to create Fm7♭5 and B♭7♯5♯9 chords before finishing off with a unison/octave line. After all this thick harmony, the unison line is a nice contrast and can sound quite powerful.

TRACK 55

The Godfather of Soul

One more chord couple that is sometimes used in minor keys comes from the world of "old school" R&B, as in James Brown. This is the kind of parallel harmony his horn section would often use. In this case, both chords of the couple are major triads. The main chord is formed by the upper three notes of a m7 chord. To get the second chord we just move the right hand up by a whole step. Here it is in D minor:

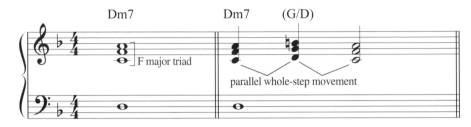

Notice how, in the following example, the same pair can also work over G7. This is a typical James Brown/ Maceo Parker vamp:

TRACK 56

This harmonization might be used for the choir, but is more likely to be used as part of an instrumental breakdown like this:

TRACK 57

Chapter 6

MELODY AND FILLS

So far we've covered a lot of ground on the subject of harmony in gospel music. But what about melody; shouldn't that have come first? Well, melody and harmony are so intertwined in gospel music that you really need a full understanding of the harmony system before you can understand its effect on melody.

Terminology

Before we get too far, let's briefly get some terminology out of the way.

As a melody moves from note to note, it can do one of three things:

1. It can move up or down to a neighboring note (an interval of either a minor 2nd or major 2nd). This is called **stepwise motion**.

2. It can move up or down by a larger interval. This is called a **leap** or **leaping motion**.

3. It can stay on the same note. This is called **static motion**.

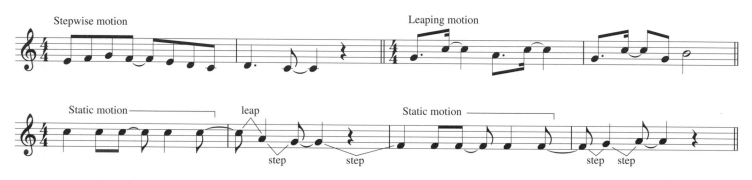

Solo melodies performed by a gospel singer or instrumentalist are usually somewhat improvised or ad lib. This means the soloist is free to use any type of melodic motion. Some scales that we'll study in the second half of this chapter can help a performer devise interesting improvisations and fills. But first, let's look at the "composed" (rather than improvised) melodies of gospel music. As we've seen throughout this book, they are often harmonized in three parts.

Melodies Harmonized in Three Parts
Limitations

All of the musical examples we've seen in previous chapters have been melodies that are harmonized in three parts. Those three parts could either be the right hand of a piano or the three parts of a choir (soprano, alto, tenor). Because they are harmonized there are some limitations on the melody. Large leaps and extremes of range, for instance, both create some problems, and so are pretty rare. Let's look at some examples to see why.

TRACK 58

This example has a large leap that would be difficult for a choir to pull off consistently. (It might even be difficult for a pianist to negotiate at a fast tempo.) All three parts jump from a comfortable part of their range into the extreme high end. The altos would have an especially hard time with an upward leap of a minor 7th. This example would be more successful if done in one of these two ways:

TRACK 59

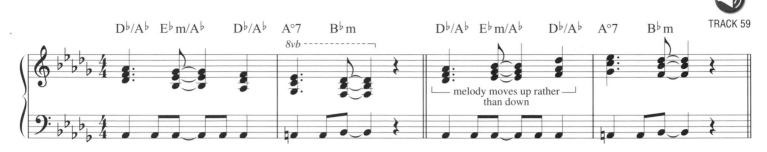

In the first revision we've moved the second measure down an octave to avoid the leap and the extreme register change. In the second revision we've changed the melody in the first measure to make it climb up gradually to the higher range.

Seasoned arrangers may also want to try this next solution for a choir arrangement.

TRACK 60

In this version the second measure uses **open** voicing rather than **close** voicing. This is accomplished by dropping the middle note of the original voicing down an octave. This results in a chord voicing that spans more than an octave. Although it does help the altos and tenors immensely, it is very uncharacteristic of gospel choir arranging. In fact, the only time I've ever encountered open voicing for the choir in gospel music is in published arrangements that are "in a gospel style." I don't ever remember hearing it in the gospel music I've transcribed from recordings.

Of course, a low register can be problematic as well. On the piano the sound can start to get somewhat muddy, and in a choir the voices don't project well at the bottom of their ranges. This next example, while certainly possible, is about at the limit for low register, especially if it is sung.

TRACK 61a

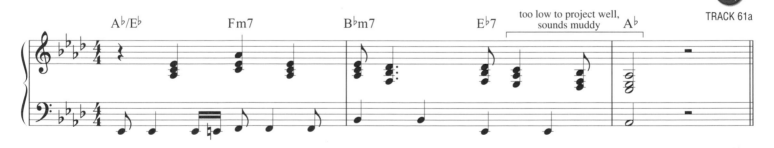

Something like this gives a similar effect and would project much better:

TRACK 61b

Stepwise Motion

Stepwise motion in the melody is handled pretty easily in gospel music by all the devices we've discussed in previous chapters. These include:

TRACK 62

Leaps by Inversion

Melodic leaps fall into a few different categories. The most common is when the melody simply leaps from one chord tone to another. This causes our three-part voicing to change inversions. In choral singing this is the easiest type of leap to hear, because the next note is already being sung by one of the other sections (although possibly in a different octave). Here's an example where the melody simply leaps from root to 3rd to 5th of the G major triad:

TRACK 63

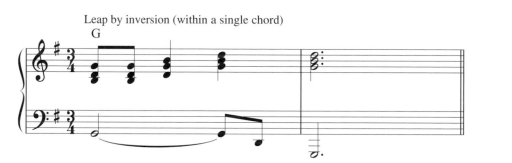

An extension of this concept is when the right hand (or choir) leaps by inversion, as in the above example, but the bass changes to create new chords. In this next example there are two leaps. At each leap the right hand continues to play a C triad, but the bass moves from C to A to F. (The C/F is basically an incomplete version of Fmaj9.)

TRACK 64

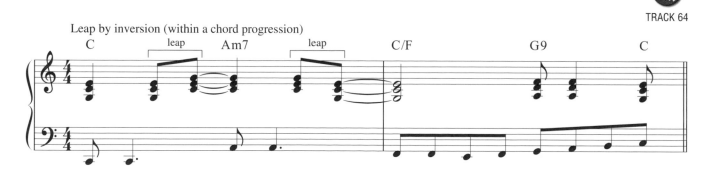

Leap Within a "Couple"

The other most common melodic leap in gospel music is between the two chords of a "couple" pair. There is already a built-in leap because the pairing covers only six of the seven notes of a major scale. Here is an example from earlier that shows how these pairs work. This time the melodic leaps are marked.

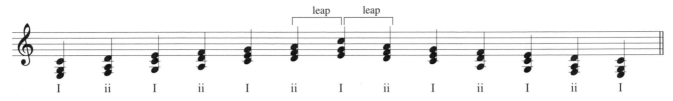

I   ii   I   ii   I   ii   I   ii   I   ii   I   ii   I

When sung, this leap is heard easily by all sections of the choir. In fact, they may not even perceive it as a leap because the sound of the six-note gospel scale is so ingrained in their hearing. Here's an example in Dᵇ:

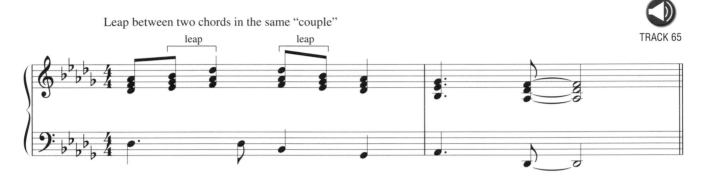

Leap between two chords in the same "couple"

TRACK 65

It's also possible to have a larger leap from one chord of a "couple" pair to the other, not just across the "missing" 7th scale degree. This next example shows one possibility. These parts might be slightly harder for a choir to hear at first, but they are still very singable. The leap is made easier to hear because the chords are in the same pair and because the leap resolves back downward in a sort of echo.

Larger leap within a chord couple

TRACK 66

Leap to a Related "Couple"

The last of the more common leaps is to a closely related "couple" pair. This could be from the I–ii pair to either the IV–v pair or the V–vi pair. In this example in Bᵇ you'll see that we start out with the I–ii couple pair (Bᵇ major and C minor triads) before leaping to an F minor triad (the v in a IV–v couple). This really pulls us to the downward resolution on the Eᵇ triad in measure 3.

TRACK 67

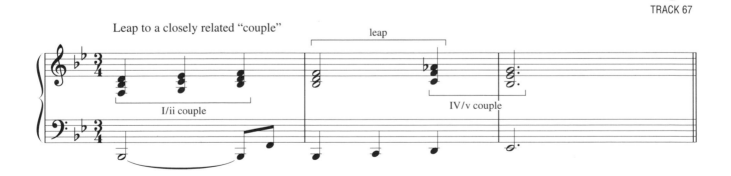

Leap to a closely related "couple"

Leap to a Backtrack Chord

Now we get to some of the less common leaps (though all are certainly used in gospel music). The first of these is the leap to a "backtrack" chord. Usually "backtrack" chords are used when melodic motion is either stepwise or static.

Here is an example in which the main chord leaps to its "backtrack" chord, which then resolves in a regular, non-leaping way (by static motion in this case).

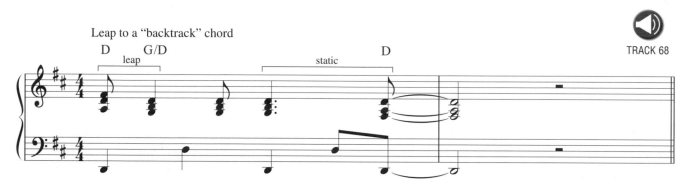

TRACK 68

Leap to a More Distant Chord

Occasionally you can even find a leap to a somewhat more distant chord. Here is an example in the style of "He's Worthy to be Praised" by the Colorado Mass Choir. It's in the key of A♭. The first phrase stays in A♭, but the second phrase ends in D♭, propelled there by a secondary ii–V progression. This wouldn't normally present a problem, but the transition coincides with a leap in the melody (a leap of a tritone, no less!). So here we have a leap to a secondary ii7:

TRACK 69

You can tell that if a choir sang this, the sopranos might have a hard time hearing their note because of the tritone leap. Additionally, the tenors may have trouble because they are making a large leap to a chromatically altered note (a note not in the key signature) near the upper limit of their range, which is also a half step from the soprano note in the previous chord and a tritone away from the C♮ the tenors just sang in measure 3. All of this combines to make this a somewhat precarious (but certainly still possible) passage. (It doesn't sit that well on the piano, either!)

Melodic Fills

There are certainly lots of opportunities to improvise and/or compose your own fills in gospel playing. Of course, common sense tells us that fills work best when they complement the melody rather than fight it. This means that fills are usually more appropriate at times when the melody is resting or sustaining a longer note. It also means that a fill that arpeggiates the current chord or uses the major (or minor) scale of the key you're currently playing in will be least likely to interfere with the melody.

Arpeggios

Here is an example using an arpeggio figure that's based on "Thank God for the Blood" by the Florida Mass Choir. Use the fingerings indicated on the arpeggios for the smoothest performance.

TRACK 70

Major-scale Runs

This next example uses a major-scale fill (measure 4) to connect the end of one section to the beginning of the next. Although this example is in the key C we will be using the F major scale (which has a B♭ instead of a B♮) because we are trying to telegraph to the singers and the audience that the next section starts on an F chord. Once we get there, we go right back to using a B♮ because we haven't actually modulated to F; we just used the F major scale to pull us there strongly.

TRACK 71

Other Melodic Figures

Here's a common fill figure in gospel music that comes from the major scale. It uses the half steps found between the 3rd and 4th or between the 7th and 1st scale degrees, followed by a perfect 5th as a sort of signature. Here are the two places you'll find it in the key of C major:

This figure can be expanded by adding a note in the middle, changing the intervals to half step, whole step, and perfect 4th.

This figure can be used over almost every diatonic (in the key signature) bass note. Let's take a look at the possibilities.

TRACK 72

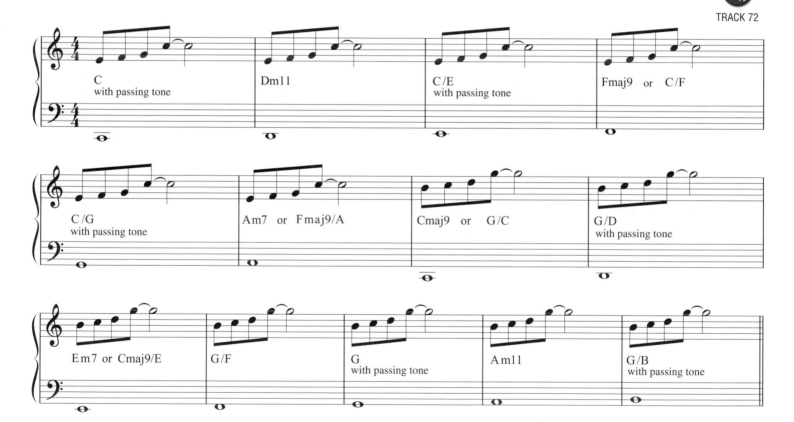

As you can see, this creates lots of harmonic possibilities with a fairly simple figure. You can also turn this figure "upside down" by starting with the upper note of the half step and going down the group of notes.

TRACK 73

Let's put this into practice. Here's an example with lots of fills using this common gospel figure:

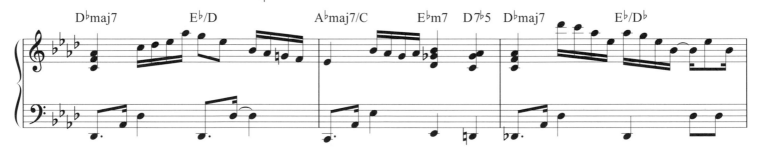

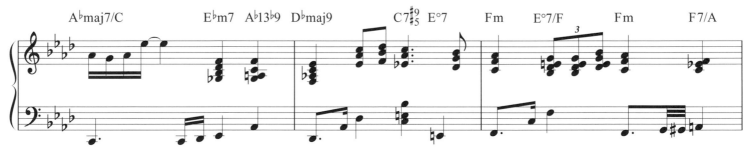

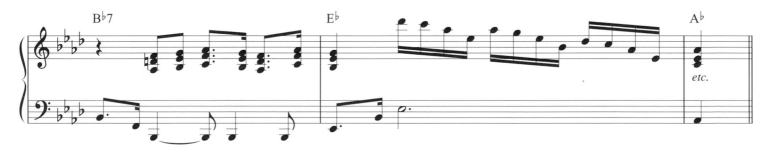

The Major and Minor Blues Scales

Another scale that gets used often in gospel music is the blues scale, although not always in the same way that it's used in other styles of music. First of all, let's review the blues scale and its variations.

Construction of Major and Minor Blues Scales

The basic blues scale comes from the pentatonic (meaning "five-note") scale, so maybe we should review that first. There are actually two pentatonic scales, major and minor. The major pentatonic scale uses the 1st, 2nd, 3rd, 5th, and 6th notes of the major scale. The 4th and 7th scale degrees are omitted. Here it is in C major:

C major pentatonic scale

scale degree: 1   2   3   5   6   1   6   5   3   2   1

If we use this same scale (the same pitches) but start on A, we get an A minor pentatonic scale. It's no coincidence that A is the **relative minor** of C major (meaning that the keys of A minor and C major share the same key signature). Notice that the scale degrees have been renumbered to start from A.

A minor pentatonic scale

scale degree: 1   3   4   5   7   1   7   5   4   3   1

By adding one note to this A minor pentatonic scale, we get the A minor blues scale. That added note is the flatted 5th scale degree (sometimes spelled as a raised 4th scale degree when it resolves upward to the natural 5th scale degree).

A minor blues scale

scale degree: 1   3   4   ♭5   5   7   1   7   5   ♭5   4   3   1

It's important to notice that, compared to the corresponding minor key, there is only one altered note in the minor blues scale (the flatted 5th scale degree). However, the minor blues scale can also be used in a standard "major" sounding blues that consists mostly of dominant seventh chords. This type of blues is always notated using the major key's signature. When comparing the minor blues scale to the major scale we find that there are three notes that are altered (lowered 3rd, 5th, and 7th).

A minor blues scale (notated within an A major key signature)

scale degree: 1   ♭3   4   ♭5   5   ♭7   1   ♭7   5   ♭5   4   ♭3   1

We can now take this scale back to C major by using the same notes, but starting on C. This scale is called the major blues scale.

C major blues scale

scale degree: 1   2   ♭3   3   5   6   1   6   5   3   ♭3   2   1

Note that when talking about blues and jazz, the term "blues scale" (without specifying major or minor) refers to the minor blues scale because it is so much more common in those styles than the major blues scale. In gospel music, however, the major blues scale is used quite frequently.

Major-blues-scale Licks

Here's a typical lick using the major blues scale:

TRACK 75

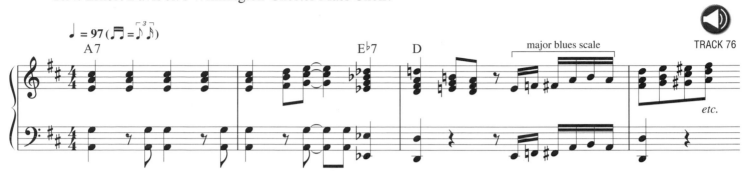

Let's hear it in context. Here's an example in the style of "It's Mighty Nice (to be on the Lord's Side)" by Rev. Ernest Davis Jr.'s Wilmington-Chester Mass Choir:

TRACK 76

Because the blues scale has six notes, it works quite well in triplet figures. It also lends itself to simple fingerings. Check out how easily the A♭ major blues scale falls under just the first three fingers in the right hand.

A♭ major blues scale fingering (right hand)

Here is an example based on "Suddenly" by Bishop Eddie L. Long. At every repeat there is a triplet-based fill using the major blues scale.

TRACK 77

Minor-blues-scale Licks

The minor blues scale can obviously be used as fill material in minor-key songs (or sections).

TRACK 78

The minor blues scale can also be used in major keys when the chord progression is blues-oriented (made up of mostly dominant seventh chords).

TRACK 79

For a more complete look at blues scales, be sure to check out Mark Harrison's excellent book *Blues Piano* in this same Hal Leonard Keyboard Style Series.

Chapter 7
FORM, FLEXIBILITY, TERMINOLOGY, AND TIME

There are some aspects of playing with a gospel choir that aren't directly related to melody, harmony, or rhythm. They are the unwritten (perhaps until now...) rules. Some are what classical musicians might call "performance practice." Others are just a result of the sometimes difficult process of communicating between musicians—some of whom usually play written music, while others keep it all in their head. Basically, these are the things I've learned in ten years of playing with gospel choirs that I wish someone would have told me on the first day.

Form and Flexibility

Let's talk about **form**. By form, I'm referring to the sections of a song and the order in which they are performed. In classical music there are some standard forms that even have names (sonata, rondo, etc.). Popular songs of the 1930s–1950s often used what came to be called "thirty-two-bar song form" (AABA). Pop songs of the last 30 or 40 years often have a very predictable form (intro, verse 1, verse 2, pre-chorus, chorus, verse 3, pre-chorus, chorus, bridge, chorus, ending).

In gospel music the form is much less predictable. There's nearly always an introduction, but the next section may be a chorus or verse. There may be verses with a common refrain at the end of each one. These verses may be musically different (even of different lengths!), but may still have the same refrain at the end. It may be hard to identify some sections with familiar terminology. What I call the bridge, the lead singer may call the "special chorus." I've played several gospel songs where the form is section 1, repeat it, section 2, repeat it, section 3, and repeat it until the end; we never go back and catch sections 1 or 2 again.

The other thing that must be understood about form in gospel music is that it is very flexible. In performance some sections may repeat more (or fewer) times than in a previous performance. You might jump back to a previous section, even if you've never rehearsed it that way.

So, how do you know what's happening next? You need to watch and listen to the choir director and/or the lead singer (which might be the same person). They may use hand signals to indicate whether to repeat or move on to the next section. Make sure you know what the signals are, because they are not standardized. An index finger pointed upwards and turned in a small circle may mean either "take it around again" or "wrap it up!"

The lead singer may also use verbal direction to indicate which section is coming next. You've probably heard James Brown shouting, "Take it to the bridge! Take it to the bridge!" But what if (as we discussed above) the sections don't have readily identifiable labels? Well, the first lyric line is what identifies each section in gospel music. So, if the lead singer wants to go back to the "bridge" he or she will sing (or say) the first lyric line (or a fragment of it) as a cue to the choir and accompanists. This will come just before the transition, so you need to be paying attention! (You also need to make sure you can hear the lead singer clearly through the P.A. system or monitors.) This same verbal technique can be used to cue in and out of repeats and endings. Sometimes the choir director or lead singer will decide to cue the accompaniment "out" and create an *a cappella* section. Usually the drums will continue playing.

Often the last section of a song will be repeated many times and modulate up by half steps. This may also be cued verbally ("Take it up! Take it up!"). The number of modulations you go through may be different from one performance to the next, depending on how tired the choir is and the level of audience reaction and energy. This means the ending may turn out to be in a different key than the one you practiced it in! You need to be able to transpose quickly on the fly or be very handy with the transpose button on your keyboard. (This is something to consider when purchasing a keyboard for use with a gospel choir. Are there dedicated up and down switches for transposing, or do you need to page through menus or otherwise stop playing to change transpose values?) If you do use a transpose switch, be sure to set it back to zero before starting the next song!

While we're on the subject of endings, be aware that a song may not be over when you think it's over. Even if the audience is applauding already, the director or lead singer may decide, "It felt so good, we can't stop now," and cue everyone back in on the last section. If it's a section that was modulating up by half steps, then don't be surprised if the "restart" is yet another half step higher. The bottom line is this: anything could happen in terms of form. Be attentive and flexible.

Terminology

We've learned that gospel music doesn't always have standardized terminology. Because the sections are identified by their lyrics, it can be difficult to pinpoint a starting location in the middle of a song when rehearsing. When dealing with written music, we can always say, "Let's start two before D" and everyone knows exactly where we are. In gospel music it's often harder to describe an exact location based on lyrics and a possibly flexible form.

Also, because the singers base their concept of the form on the lyrics, there is often miscommunication regarding the numbering of repeats. For instance, in the following example the accompanists would agree with the notation on the sheet music that this section is played four times. The singers, however, would likely say that this section repeats 16 times, because that's how many times they sing the word "faith."

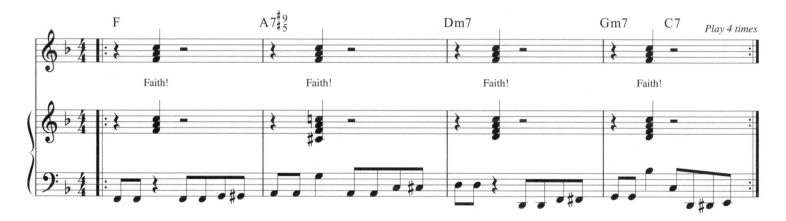

(Incidentally, this kind of confusion concerning numbering repeats isn't unique to gospel music. Try working with a choreographer sometime!)

There are some techniques that don't have a directly equivalent term in classical music. One is the **circle**. In a circle the sections of the choir cycle through their notes to create a different texture. Let's take our previous example from above and do a circle.

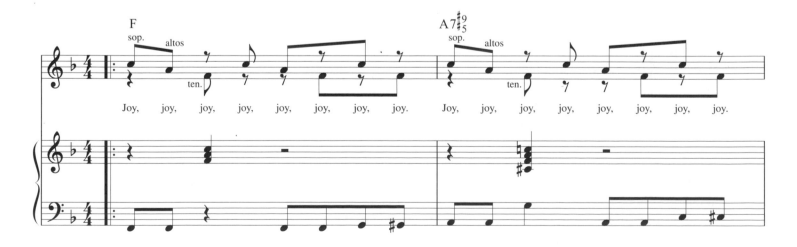

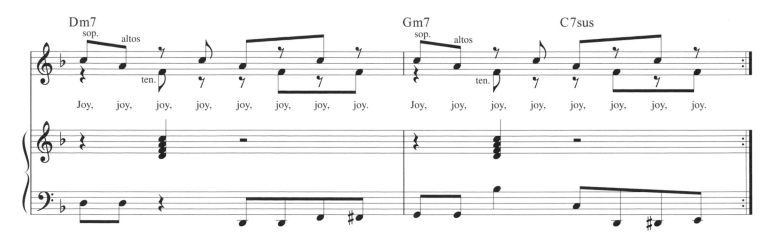

This effect was made popular by Kirk Franklin and the Family in their modernized version of the classic hymn "Jesus Paid It All" from the album *Whatcha Lookin' 4*.

Another common technique is an inversion change in the choir parts. A fairly short section (say, four measures) is repeated a couple of times. Then, to add energy, each of the sections moves up one part. The tenors begin singing the alto notes, the altos begin singing the soprano notes, and the sopranos begin singing the tenor notes up an octave. Here's an example:

Notice that in the second line all the vocal parts have moved up to create a higher inversion of the first line. I'm not aware of a standard term for this technique. I have, unfortunately, heard it on occasion mistakenly called a "key change." I think this is because the parts go higher in order to create more energy (which a "key change/half-step modulation" also does). I call it an **inversion change**.

Time Feel

Like any highly rhythmic music, gospel music needs to "groove" to sound right, and that depends to a large extent on the accompanists. Time and feel are critical. If you are accompanying a gospel choir with just a piano (no band), you have to become the full band. You need to add little ghost notes that fill in the rhythmic subdivisions that would otherwise be provided by a drummer. Feel free to change a written part to help provide a consistent and unmistakable groove. Have the choir clap on beats 2 and 4 to provide the backbeat. Make sure the choir and the piano aren't too far apart, especially if you don't have monitor speakers. The distance can create time issues/delays.

On slow ballads make sure not to rush. The tempo may seem uncomfortably slow at first, but the singers need the time for all the inflections and bends they want to do. This is difficult without a drummer. Keep thinking of the smallest subdivision (usually sixteenth notes on a ballad) so you don't unconsciously pick up the tempo. Nothing will get you a dirty look quicker than rushing a singer through a ballad!

Chapter 8
PUTTING IT TOGETHER: STYLES AND GROOVES

Like any other type of music, gospel has a staple of styles and grooves that it draws upon. Let's look at the main styles and grooves using all of the knowledge we've gained from the previous chapters.

Up-tempo Shuffle

The up-tempo shuffle is the style that pops into most people's heads when you say "gospel music." It's the "hand-clappin'-foot-stompin'-dancin'-in-the-aisles" feel that everybody loves.

It's definitely "up-tempo" because this style is usually played somewhere between 190-240 beats per minute. It's called a "shuffle" because the eighth notes are swung (or "shuffled"), meaning that the offbeat eighth notes are all slightly late. You'll often find the following symbol at the beginning of a song with swing eighth notes as we've seen in many songs so far.

$$\left(\sqcap = \overset{\ulcorner 3 \urcorner}{\rfloor \, \flat} \right)$$

This tells you that the offbeat eighth notes should be placed where the last note of an eighth-note triplet would be placed. This is basically correct, since you'll often find eighth-note triplets mixed in with swing/ shuffle styles, although the finer points of placing swing eighth notes depend somewhat on tempo and style. Generally speaking, at faster tempos the eighth notes straighten back out somewhat.

In a similar fashion to jazz and swing music, the bass notes (supplied either by a bassist, or by the pianist's left hand) will "walk" on quarter notes for much of the time, stopping only to play the accented "kicks" and syncopated figures. The right hand is constantly going back and forth between "on-beat" and "off-beat" figures that help propel the music forward. All of the syncopations are anticipations rather than delayed figures.

When playing the following tune with just piano, it's important to keep the walking bass going (in a full rhythm section the bass player can, of course, cover much of it). Harmonically, this song uses almost all the techniques we've discussed in just the first eight measures. You'll find a "trio" group in measures 1–2 (I–ii–♭III), backtracking in measure 3, chromatic parallels in measure 4, a secondary dominant in measure 5, and altered secondary dominants in measures 7–8. This style is closely related to the blues (note the unison/ octave figures using the minor blues scale in measures 25–26, 48, and 57–58), so you'll find lots of dominant 7th chords, fewer minor 7th chords, and almost no major 7th chords. You'll also see a half-step modulation at the end. In a real-life situation that section would likely continue to go up by half steps until some of the vocalists began to pass out. In this situation you need to be able to transpose at sight (or be handy with the transpose button on your keyboard).

TRACK 80
full mix

TRACK 81
minus piano

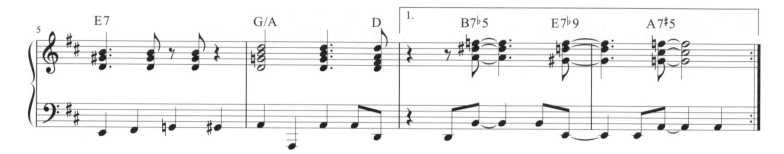

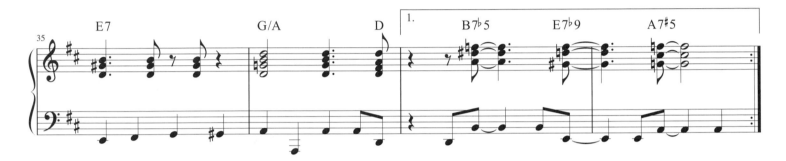

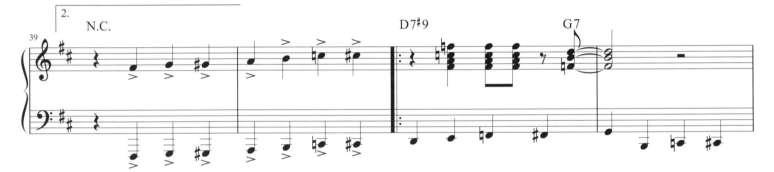

Slow Ballad

At the opposite extreme lies the slow ballad. In pop music, ballads are seldom much slower than about 58–60 beats per minute. Often in gospel music, however, the slow ballad drops into the range of 44–56 beats per minute. This can become quite a balancing act for the keyboardist. If you let the tempo speed up, the singer loses space for expression, yet the song begins to die if the tempo drags too much. Try to keep the sixteenth-note subdivision going in your head at all times (even when you're playing eighth and quarter notes). This will keep the temptation to rush in check.

Slow ballads are always sixteenth-note based and do not swing or shuffle. They usually still have anticipated syncopations, which may be difficult to feel at first when the tempo is so slow. Although they usually start at a quiet dynamic, slow ballads can get pretty big and can have sudden dynamic changes or loud attention-grabbing hits. Harmonically, the slow ballad has more opportunity for colorful chords than the up-tempo shuffle, simply because of the slower harmonic rhythm (the pace at which the chords change) and the fact that the slow ballad is not so blues-based.

Often there's a two-, four-, or eight-measure section near the end that repeats until the lead singer or director cues everyone to go to the ending. This section has the potential to build to a peak over many repeats. It allows the lead singer to improvise freely while the rhythm section builds in both volume and excitement. Sometimes writing out this repeat can get tricky because the repeat may go back to a measure that is not the beginning of a phrase or the repeat may require a transition to get into it and a different transition to get out of it. In the example you'll see that the repeat starts at measure 21, even though measure 22 is actually the beginning of the four-bar phrase.

TRACK 82
full mix

TRACK 83
minus piano

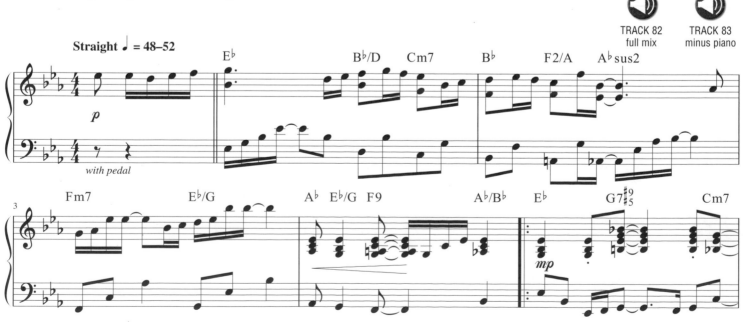

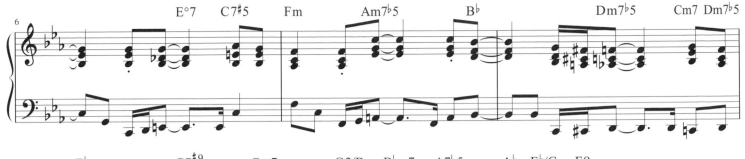

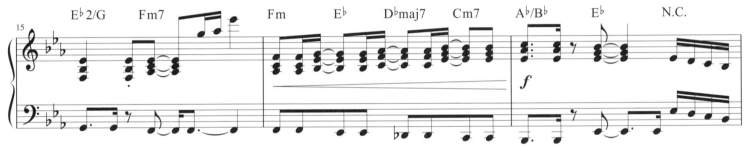

Triple-meter Gospel Waltz (3/4 and 6/8)

I'm somewhat hesitant to call this style "gospel waltz," since "waltz" really refers to a specific dance, not just triple meter in general. Regardless, it is sometimes referred to that way. It's sometimes notated in 3/4 time with swing eighth notes and sometimes in 6/8 time with swing sixteenth notes. The other reason for my disagreement with the term has to do with placement of the backbeat (the snare-drum hit that falls on beats 2 and 4 in 4/4 time). In a traditional waltz the "backbeat" falls on beat 2 and 3, like this:

But in a gospel waltz the backbeat falls on beat 1 of the second measure, in what amounts to a "half-time" feel.

Because this feels like a *single* unit that actually spans two measures, some prefer to notate this style in 6/8 time, with each measure taking the time of two 3/4 measures.

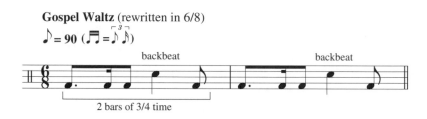

In the following example you can see how the "couple" chords in the introduction lend themselves easily to **contrary motion** between the hands (i.e., the hands move in opposite directions). There are a few small fills (and one big one at measure 41). Some of them just arpeggiate chord tones (measure 10), while others use the major blues scale (measures 23 and 41, for example). Notice also how the F°7 chord in measure 55 sets us on a path back to the A/E so the section can repeat. Compare this to measure 22, where the same phrase ends without repeats.

TRACK 84
full mix

TRACK 85
minus piano

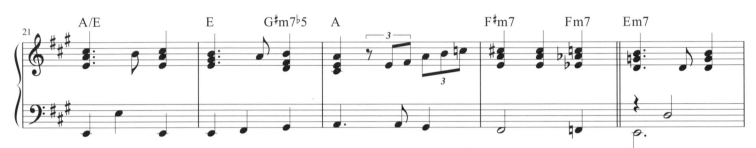

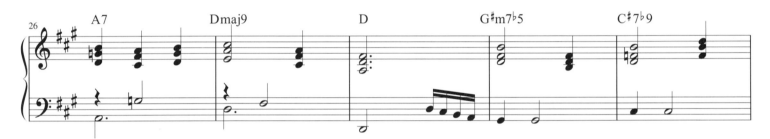

Sixteenth-note Shuffle (or Half-time Shuffle)

This is a shuffle type of groove where it's the sixteenth notes, rather than eighth notes, that are swung (shuffled). Tempos for this style typically don't go much beyond 100 beats per minute. A typical drum groove might look like this:

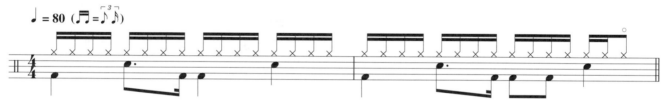

This groove is sometimes called a "half-time" shuffle. The name has nothing to do with basketball. It came about because if you notate it with shuffled eighth notes at double the beats per minute, the snare-drum backbeat ends up on beat 3 of each measure instead of beats 2 and 4. Here is the same pattern re-written to show the "half-time" snare notes on beat three:

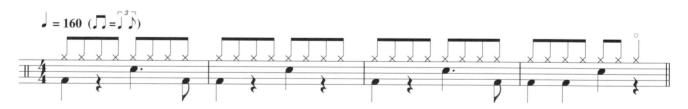

In the next example you'll notice that the whole piano part isn't filled with sixteenth notes (like you might expect from a groove called "sixteenth-note shuffle"). They appear in the bass line (measures 1–3) and in the right-hand figure in measures 17, 19, and 21. Otherwise, much of the shuffle in this feel comes from the drummer and the use of the hi-hat. If this is played without a drummer, you may need to add some ghost notes that hint more at the underlying sixteenth-note subdivision.

Note how catchy the syncopated figure is in measures 5–6. Also take note of the A7#5#9 chord in measure 2. If sung, the tenors would sing the C♮, but the pianist can sneak in the C# as well to change the chord from a simple F/A to the more colorful A7#5#9. This also helps bring us to the Dm chord in measure 3, since A7 is V of Dm. Measures 25–32 are more of an interlude during which a solo singer might improvise; the piano part here is more fill and chord outline than composed harmonized melody.

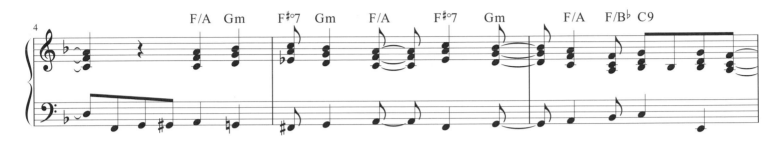

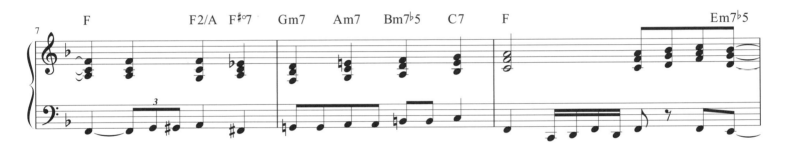

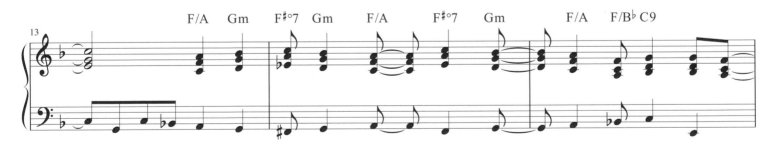

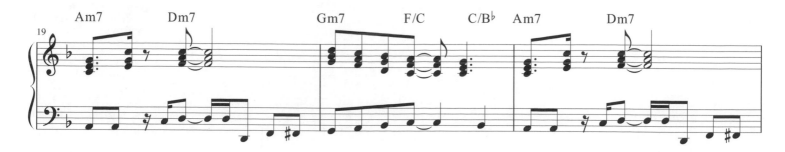

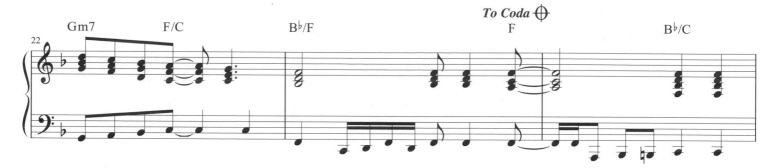

A sixteenth-note shuffle can also be used to create a more modern hip-hop/R&B type of groove (especially when used in a minor key).

Straight-sixteenth feel

The straight sixteenth-note feel is probably the furthest we get from "old-school" gospel. These grooves often display the influence of Latin and R&B/funk music. Our upcoming song definitely has a Latin flavor. I can definitely imagine the syncopated line in the introduction being played by brassy trumpets (or a keyboard producing a tamer imitation).

Three-against-four Figures

In a measure of 4/4 time we normally have four groups of four sixteenth notes each.

In a "three-against-four" pattern we arrange the sixteenth notes in groups of three (and some twos or fours to make the pattern come back to beat one). You'll see in the following examples some of the different possibilities. The numbers above each chord or rest show how many sixteenth notes it is equal to.

TRACK 88

Circle of 5ths

Measures 20–23 also demonstrate another common device used in gospel music, the **circle of 5ths**. The roots of the chord progression go through the circle of 5ths as follows: A, D, G, C, F, B♭, and E♭. The E♭ then goes back to A, an interval of a diminished 5th.

TRACK 89
full mix

TRACK 90
minus piano

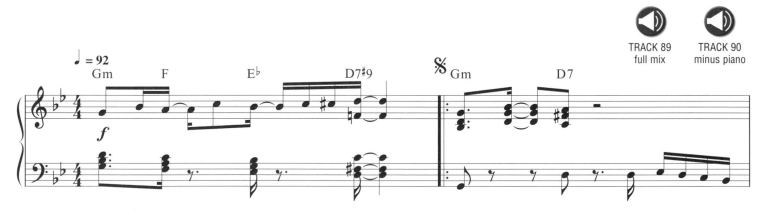

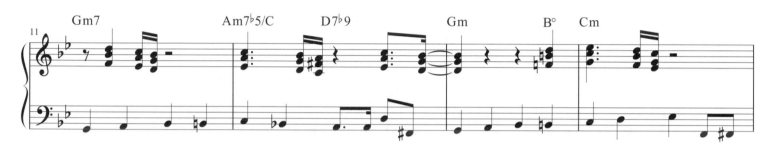

Medium-tempo Shuffle

The medium-tempo shuffle is a staple of more traditional gospel music. It feels good and is easy to stand up and clap along with. It sits at a tempo where swing eighth notes and eighth note triplets both fall comfortably.

The intro figure in the next example uses eighth-note triplets and the major blues scale. Although this song doesn't use a blues chord progression, the first section does happen to be twelve bars long. It uses the extended "couple" (parallel chords) to give that bluesy sound in measures 3–4. The backtrack figure in measure 13 also reinforces the blues flavor. The big F7♯9 chord (secondary dominant: V of B♭) really pulls us to B♭m to start the next section. The B♭7 (instead of B♭m) at measure 29 starts the move back through E♭ to A♭. This is dramatized by a return of the intro figure at measure 33, which adds an extra two bars to the section, reinforcing the dominant E♭ in the bass and heightening expectation for the arrival of A♭ at measure 3. At measure 37, B♭7 is used again, although this time it takes us only as far as E♭ (the whole section at measures 38–49 is really in the key of E♭). The intro figure (measures 52–53) again brings us back to restate the first section and end the song.

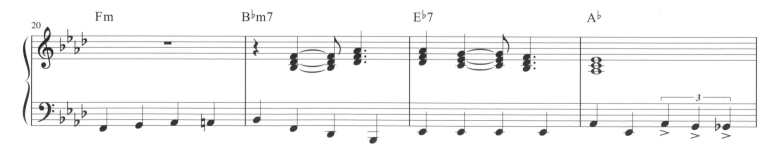

D.S. al Coda

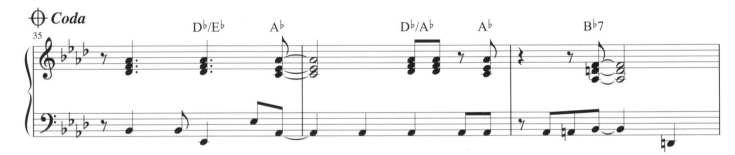

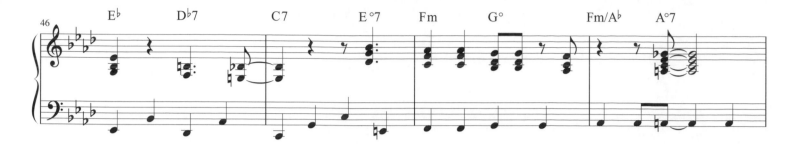

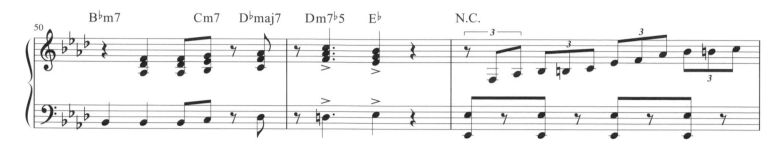

Straight-eighth Feel

This is more of a "pop music" feel that can sometimes stray into almost pop/jazz/rock fusion. The three-part harmony is what keeps it solidly gospel, especially the use of the ii° chord. Notice how many times the note A is altered to A♭ because of the ii° chord in the first section of the song (measures 9–16). In this first section, the piano outlines the harmony that would be sung by the choir. In the other sections (measures 17–24 and 35–50), the piano plays "hits" that outline the harmony and chord progression. The choir or soloist would sing (either in three-part harmony or in unison) a more legato line that contrasts with the punches in the rhythm section. Measures 33–34 are a more adventurous type of transition (which is becoming more and more common in gospel music) using parallel motion combined with jazz/fusion harmonies. These two bars would be strictly instrumental.

TRACK 93
full mix

TRACK 94
minus piano

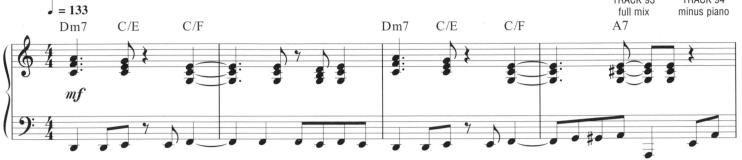

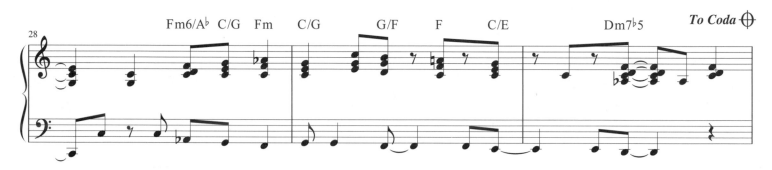

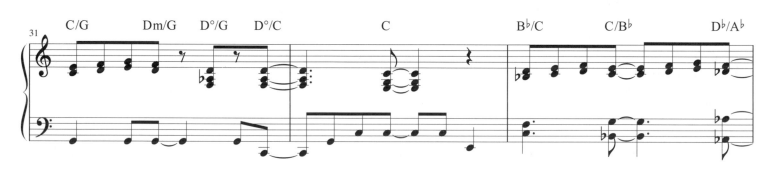

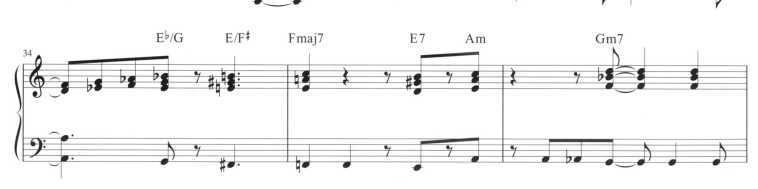

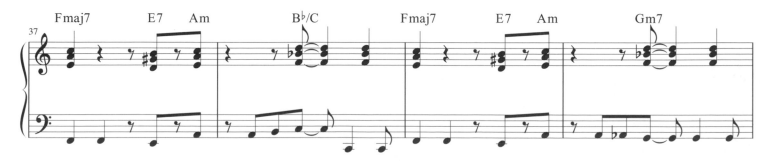

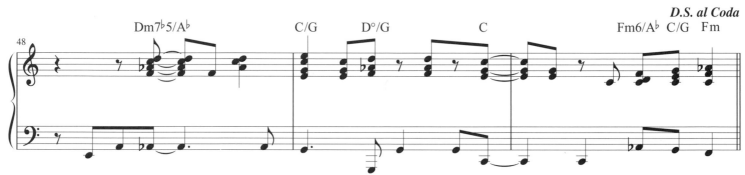

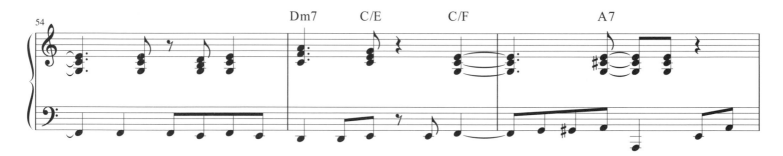

LISTENING LIST

Here is a short list of gospel artists that most closely reflect the content of this book:

Colorado Mass Choir (w/Joe Pace)

Donnie McClurkin

Fred Hammond (and Radical for Christ)

L.A. Mass Choir

Georgia Mass Choir

Hezekiah Walker (and the Love Fellowship Choir)

John P. Kee

Kirk Franklin (and the Family)

Kurt Carr

Marvin Sapp

Mississippi Mass Choir

New Direction

Norman Hutchins

Rev. Milton Brunson

Richard Smallwood (and Vision)

Ricky Dillard

The New Life Community Choir

Walter Hawkins

V.I.P. Mass Choir